ideals
Naturally Nutritious
COOKBOOK

by Donna M. Paananen

Natural foods are ideal because they are not only the healthiest foods but they taste better than those commercially refined.

If you are concerned about your own health and the health of those you love, if you are tired of expensive "convenience" food products chock-full of additives, and if you are willing to spend a little time to provide interesting, delicious, and nutritious foods for those who eat at your table, then this book is for you.

Natural foods are the kind our great-grandparents used when they cooked "from scratch." Whole wheat flour, wheat germ, honey, brown rice, old-fashioned molasses, and other wholesome foods have recently made their comeback, much to the benefit of those of us who use them in our cookery.

The upsurge of interest in growing one's own food contributes to natural nutrition as well. If you are already growing some of your own fruits and vegetables, you know the joy of fresh, garden-ripened foods. Many recipes in this book have been chosen to utilize these home-grown vegetables as well as home-canned and home-frozen foods.

Do enjoy making your own breads, sauces, soups, snacks, desserts, etc. Please be happy, be experimental, be relaxed, and be imaginative while you cook. In the hands of the person who prepares food for a household rest the privilege and responsiblity of providing good-tasting, health-maintaining foods. Can there be a more important job?

the author

An *ideals* Publication

ISBN 0-89542-605-6 295

Contents

OTHER COOKBOOKS AVAILABLE

QUICK & SIMPLE COOKBOOK
MENUS FROM AROUND THE WORLD
CHRISTMAS GIFTS FROM THE KITCHEN
SIMPLY DELICIOUS
FROM MAMA'S KITCHEN
SOPHIE KAY'S FAMILY COOKBOOK
THE IDEALS AMERICAN COOKBOOK
THE IDEALS COUNTRY KITCHEN COOKBOOK
THE IDEALS CHRISTMAS COOKBOOK
THE IDEALS AROUND THE WORLD COOKBOOK
THE IDEALS OUTDOOR COOKBOOK
THE IDEALS ALL HOLIDAYS COOKBOOK
THE IDEALS FAMILY GARDEN COOKBOOK
THE IDEALS FAMILY COOKBOOK, VOL. 1
THE IDEALS FAMILY COOKBOOK, VOL. 2
GOURMET ON THE GO
THE IDEALS FAMILY DESSERT COOKBOOK
THE IDEALS WHOLE GRAIN COOKBOOK
THE IDEALS COMPLETE FAMILY COOKBOOK
THE IDEALS COOKIE COOKBOOK
THE IDEALS FESTIVE PARTY COOKBOOK
SOUPS FOR ALL SEASONS
THE IDEALS JUNIOR CHEF COOKBOOK

DEDICATION

To my mother, Marjorie Earle Jones, and my grandmother, the late Elsie Brom Earle, in whose kitchens I first experienced the pleasures of cookery.

photo stylist
Marybeth Owens

artwork by
Lorraine Wells

designed by
Marybeth Owens

Editorial Director, James Kuse
Managing Editor, Ralph Luedtke
Production Editor/Manager, Richard Lawson
Photographic Editor, Gerald Koser

Pictured opposite
Mackerel Mousse, p. 5

Appetizers and Savory Snacks

AVOCADO-EGG MAYONNAISE
Yield: 4 servings

4 hard-boiled eggs
1 ripe avocado
½ c. mayonnaise
Salt
Freshly ground black pepper
Crisp lettuce leaves
3 T. minced parsley
Paprika (optional)

Halve each egg lengthwise and place yolks in a small bowl. Mash yolks with pastry blender, fork, or place in blender. Peel and mash half the avocado with the yolks until mixture is smooth. Stir in ¼ cup mayonnaise (more or less as desired). Taste and add salt and pepper if necessary. Fill the egg halves and place, yolk side down, on lettuce leaves. Mix or blend the remaining avocado with the remaining mayonnaise until smooth and of desired consistency. Correct seasonings. Cover each half egg with a spoonful of the mayonnaise mixture and dust with parsley and paprika. Chill before serving.

Note: You can also slice the second half of the avocado instead of blending it into mayonnaise and use the slices as a garnish. Dip in lemon juice to prevent discoloring and cover to keep air out if you won't be serving the dish right away.

OLIVE-NUT CHEESE BALL
Yield: about 1¼ cups spread

8 oz. cream cheese, softened
¼ c. blue cheese
12 stuffed green olives, thinly sliced
½ c. chopped walnuts

Thoroughly mix together first three ingredients. Form into a ball and roll in chopped walnuts. Chill. Serve as a spread with whole wheat crackers or small rounds.

STUFFED MUSHROOMS
Yield: 1 lb. stuffed mushrooms

1 lb. fairly large mushrooms
Butter or margarine
1 medium onion, minced
¾ c. (6 oz.) braunschweiger (liverwurst)
¼ c. raw wheat germ

Preheat oven to 350°. Wash and stem mushrooms, reserving stems for stew, soup, or other purpose. Pat mushrooms dry with toweling; and, with buttered hands, thoroughly butter each mushroom. Place mushrooms stem side up on greased cooking sheet. Put braunschweiger through a grinder (with onion) if it is not already smooth and easy to handle. Mix together onion, onion juices, and meat. Stir in wheat germ. Spoon meat mixture into mushroom caps, covering generously with the stuffing. Bake for 10 minutes or until mushrooms are tender. Serve hot. Can be made ahead and refrigerated until ready to bake.

CHEESE STRAWS
Yield: 2-3 dozen

1 c. whole wheat pastry flour
½ t. salt
¼ c. margarine or butter
⅓ c. grated sharp cheddar cheese
1 t. ice water

Preheat oven to 350°. Mix flour and salt together. With a pastry blender, cut in margarine until mixture resembles crumbs. Blend in grated cheese. Add ice water, form into a ball and roll out on lightly floured cloth with a covered rolling pin, also lightly floured. Roll out approximately ¼ inch thick. Cut into 3-inch strips, ½ inch wide. Bake on ungreased baking sheet for 10 minutes or until lightly browned. Serve hot or cold. Can be made ahead and refrigerated, covered, until ready to bake.

BEST BARBECUED MEATBALLS
Yield: About 30 appetizers

1 lb. hamburger
1 medium onion, minced
¼ c. raw wheat germ
½ t. salt
   Freshly ground black pepper
1 egg, beaten
¼ c. whole wheat bread crumbs
1 T. butter

Mix together all ingredients, except butter, lightly but thoroughly. Form into bite-sized balls. In a large frying pan, brown balls in butter, adding more butter if necessary. Pour Sauce over meatballs and simmer, covered, until meat is well done and thoroughly flavored. Add dry red wine if sauce is too thick. Serve hot in a chafing dish or similar container, garnished with parsley, if desired. Serve with toothpicks.

SAUCE

1 6-oz. can tomato paste
⅓ c. water
1 T. brown sugar
1 t. wine vinegar
½ t. oregano
½ t. basil
1 large clove garlic, minced
1 t. Worcestershire sauce
1 t. old-fashioned molasses
1/16 t. cayenne pepper
   Dry red wine (optional)
   Parsley, minced

Combine all ingredients in a medium-size heavy pan. Cook gently until well-flavored. Taste and correct seasonings.

STUFFED BRUSSELS SPROUTS
Yield: About 3 dozen

1 lb. Brussels sprouts
3 oz. cream cheese (softened)
2 T. chives
½ t. Worcestershire sauce
   Salt
   Freshly ground black pepper
   Paprika

Steam Brussels sprouts until tender. Cool. Hollow out each slightly from the top. Mix together cream cheese, chives, and Worcestershire sauce. Chop the centers of the Brussels sprouts; mix into cream cheese mixture. Add salt and pepper to taste. Fill each sprout with part of the mixture. Garnish with paprika and parsley, if desired.

MACKEREL MOUSSE
Yield: Spread for over 100 crackers
or salad for 6

1 15-oz. can mackerel
1 envelope unflavored gelatin
½ c. mayonnaise
½ c. sour cream
1 t. dill weed (more or less, to taste)
1 T. horseradish
1 T. lemon juice
½ t. Worcestershire sauce
¼ t. salt
   Few drops liquid hot pepper sauce
½ c. celery, finely chopped
¼ c. green pepper, finely chopped
¼ c. pimiento, chopped (optional)

Drain mackerel, reserving liquid. Carefully remove skin and bones. Flake. Pour reserved liquid into a small saucepan; sprinkle gelatin over. Place over moderately low heat, stirring constantly until gelatin is dissolved. Remove from heat. In a large bowl, combine mayonnaise, sour cream, and seasonings. Stir in gelatin mixture. Finally fold in mackerel and vegetables. Correct seasonings. Rinse a 4-cup fish mold with cold water. Gently pour mixture into mold. Chill until firm. Unmold by dipping mold into hot water for a few seconds. Loosen the edge of the mold with the tip of a knife. Place on a bed of greens and garnish with slices of stuffed olives, parsley, and radish roses, as desired. You can also use pimiento strips as a decorative garnish.

GUACAMOLE
Yield: ¾ cup

1 t. lemon juice
¼ c. sour cream or real mayonnaise
   (see index)
2 cloves garlic
1 T. onion
¼ t. chili powder or liquid hot sauce or hot green chili pepper (to taste)
1 ripe avocado, peeled and pitted
   Salt

In order listed, place all ingredients in blender container. Run on high speed until smooth, pushing ingredients down toward the blade while blending. Pour mixture into serving bowl and cover tightly to keep air out (which will make it discolor). Chill before serving with corn chips, rye crackers, or raw vegetables, as desired.

VEGETABLE PATÉ
Yield: 1 quart

Water
¼ lb. whole wheat bread, cubed
1 large carrot, sliced
2 onions, chopped
1 T. sesame oil or vegetable oil
2 c. cooked lentils
1½ t. dill seed
3 T. fresh parsley, finely chopped
3 T. chives, finely chopped
1 sprig thyme, chopped *or* ¼ t. dry
½ t. sea or iodized salt
1 T. miso (soybean paste)
1 T. tahini (ground, hulled sesame seeds)

Soak bread in ½ cup water. In a large skillet over medium heat, sauté carrot in hot oil for about 5 minutes. Add onions and continue to sauté for about 10 minutes. Stir regularly. Add the soaked bread cubes and continue to cook and stir for about 15 minutes or until vegetables are just tender. Place lentils, dill seed, parsley, chives, and thyme into a blender. When well blended, stir into bread mixture. Stir in the rest of the ingredients; cover and simmer gently for 10 minutes. Preheat oven to 350°. Taste and correct seasonings. Pour mixture into a 1-quart mold and bake for 30 minutes. Garnish with parsley and serve with bread rounds or as you would any pâté.

ROASTED SUNFLOWER SEEDS

Seeds
Vegetable oil
Salt

Spread sunflower seeds on large baking sheet and toast in a preheated 300° oven for about 10 minutes. Drizzle with oil, sprinkle with salt, and turn. Continue to toast, stirring often, for 30 minutes more or until crisp as desired.

ROASTED PUMPKIN OR SQUASH SEEDS

Seeds
Salt
Water

Wash seeds well and soak in salted water for 48 hours. Drain and spread on a baking sheet. Roast in a 250° oven until crisp as desired, approximately 45 minutes, turning seeds every 15 minutes or so. Store in an airtight container.

LIVER PATÉ
Yield: About 3 cups

1 T. vegetable oil
1 large carrot, thinly sliced
1 large onion, thinly sliced
1 lb. beef liver, trimmed and sliced
1 clove garlic
Freshly ground black pepper
1 t. salt
¼ t. ground sage
1 T. dry sherry (optional)
3 T. margarine or butter (at room temperature)
⅓ c. non-instant powdered milk
Fresh, chopped parsley

In large skillet over medium heat, sauté carrot in oil for 5 minutes. Add onion and sauté until transparent. Turn heat to low. Gently lay liver slices on top of the vegetables and cook, covered, until liver is tender (about 10 to 12 minutes). Grind liver, vegetables, and garlic and add seasonings. Stir margarine and powdered milk into ground mixture. Add sherry. Form into a ball, chill. Before serving, sprinkle parsley over the surface. Goes well with rye bread rounds.

ALY'S RYE CRACKERS
Yield: 5-6 dozen

2 c. rye flour
½ c. soy flour
½ c. wheat germ
6 T. brown sugar
½ c. non-instant powdered milk
1 t. salt
2 T. baking powder
1 c. butter, at room temperature
½ c. milk
Whole wheat flour
Caraway, sesame, and/or poppy seeds

Mix first 7 dry ingredients together. Add butter and mix with pastry blender. Add milk and mix thoroughly. If dough is too wet, add a little whole wheat flour. Form dough into a rough ball. Preheat oven to 350°. Roll out dough on a well-floured board with a well-floured rolling pin to ⅛-inch thickness. Cut into rounds and place on buttered baking sheet. Prick lightly with a fork. Then sprinkle with caraway, sesame, and/or poppy seeds. Lightly press the seeds into the dough. Bake 10 minutes. Turn crackers over and bake 5 more minutes. Watch carefully so they don't burn; they seem to darken as they cool. Cool on wire racks. These can be frozen successfully or kept in an airtight container.

Mixed Bean Soup, p. 15
Cucumber Soup, p. 12
Pistou, p. 12

CORN CHIPS
Yield: About 6 dozen chips

2 c. cornmeal
1 c. whole wheat pastry flour
Water
Sea salt

Thoroughly mix together cornmeal and flour. Stir in water very gradually until mixture is of the right consistency to roll. Roll the dough on a lightly floured board with a lightly floured rolling pin. Cut into 1½-inch squares. Heat about a quart of vegetable oil in a deep fryer to 350°. Drop the squares a few at a time into the hot oil and fry until golden. Drain on paper toweling and sprinkle with a little salt.

RAW VEGETABLE SUGGESTIONS FOR DIPPERS

White mushrooms, cleaned
Radishes
Baby Brussels sprouts
Cucumber fingers
Frozen asparagus spears, thawed
Unpeeled zucchini slices
Unpeeled summer squash fingers
Cauliflower florets
Green pepper strips
Carrot sticks, well scrubbed
Celery sticks
Edible pod peas
Steamed green beans, tops and tails
    removed
Green onions
Baby tomatoes

Wash vegetables carefully and quickly, using the coldest water possible. Drain immediately, dry thoroughly, and store in vegetable crisper. Chill as quickly as possible and keep chilled until just before serving.

PINE NUT DIP
Yield: 4 servings

6 oz. pine nuts, chopped
½ c. plain yogurt or sour cream
Parsley, minced

Place nuts into a small bowl; gradually spoon in yogurt or sour cream by tablespoonfuls until of desired consistency. Garnish the top with parsley; cover and chill. Serve with raw vegetables.

HOT CHEESE DIP
Yield: 6 servings

½ lb. sharp cheddar cheese, grated
2 slices bacon, cooked and crumbled
1 c. finely chopped onion

Preheat oven to 400°. Place grated cheese into a small baking dish. Stir in bacon and onion. Bake for 20 minutes or until cheese bubbles. Place dish in center of a large heat-proof tray and surround with rye crackers, corn chips, etc.

HOUMMOUS
(Chick-pea dip)
Yield: About 3 cups

2 c. well cooked chick-peas, drained
    (save liquid)
1 c. tahini*, stirred until smooth
½ c. lemon juice
6 cloves garlic
½ c. chick-pea liquid
2 t. salt (to taste)

Place ingredients in blender; blend until smooth. (In some blenders it might be best to make half a batch at a time.) Correct seasonings. Chill. Serve in a large bowl; garnish with chopped fresh parsley. Good with pita bread (pocket bread) and fresh vegetables such as carrot sticks, radishes, cucumber sticks, celery sticks, zucchini slices, green and red pepper strips.

Note: Sometimes this dish is garnished with whole chick-peas, paprika, cayenne pepper, or a combination of these.

*ground hulled sesame seeds

CHICK-PEAS

Chick-peas, another name for garbanzo beans, can be cooked using the same methods as for dried beans. Rinse and pick over the chick-peas; cover with at least twice as much water and let stand overnight. Cook the next day until tender; depending upon the quality of the chick-peas, this can take up to four hours. To shorten preparation time, cover the chick-peas with cold water, bring them to a boil, simmer for two minutes. Then let stand, tightly covered for 2 hours — away from the heat. Continue cooking until tender.

Soups and Juices

BEEF STOCK
Yield: About 2 quarts

2-3 lbs. leftover beef and bones, scraps, and/or fresh beef shanks, marrow bones, etc.
2 qts. water or vegetable cooking liquid
1 t. salt
4 peppercorns
1 large onion, studded with 4 cloves
1 bay leaf
1 c. scrubbed, chopped carrot
½ c. chopped celery
3 sprigs parsley
1 sprig thyme *or* ⅛ t. dry
1 small turnip, scrubbed and chopped (optional)

Bring meat, bones, water, and salt to a boil in a large soup kettle or Dutch oven. Skim surface regularly; cover and simmer 15 minutes. Add the rest of the ingredients; cover and let simmer 3 to 5 hours or until stock is well-flavored and of desired consistency. Taste and correct seasonings. Cool and strain. (Skim off fat.) Stock can be frozen, if desired. Meat can be used in another recipe.

CHICKEN STOCK
Yield: About 4 cups stock

1 cooked chicken carcass (with leftover skin and meat)
Giblets
1 c. chopped onion
½ c. chopped celery
1 bay leaf
¼ c. chopped parsley
7 peppercorns
⅛ t. thyme (1 sprig, if fresh)
Salt
Freshly ground black pepper

Place chicken carcass and giblets into a large pan with vegetables and seasonings (except pepper and salt). Cover with water. Slowly bring to boil. Turn down heat and simmer, covered, 1 to 2 hours or until meat falls off the bones and stock is well flavored. Strain. Add salt and pepper to taste. Use immediately or freeze for later use.

VEGETABLE BROTH
Yield: About 3½ quarts stock

2 c. chopped onion
2 c. scrubbed and chopped carrots
1 c. leeks, cleaned and chopped
1½ c. chopped celery
½ c. scrubbed and chopped turnip (optional)
1 T. margarine or vegetable oil
2 qts. water or vegetable cooking liquid
7 peppercorns
1 bay leaf
6 sprigs parsley
1 sprig thyme (or ⅛ t. dry)
Salt
Freshly ground black pepper

In a large skillet or Dutch oven, brown vegetables in oil until golden. Add water, seasonings, and herbs. Bring to a boil, turn heat down and simmer, covered, 1½ to 2 hours. Strain stock and use immediately or freeze.

MUSHROOM BROTH
Yield: 6-8 servings

¼ c. butter or margarine
¾ lb. mushrooms, cleaned and thinly sliced
⅓ c. minced onion
1 clove garlic, minced
2 T. lemon juice (*or* dry, white wine)
5-6 c. beef stock or broth
Salt
Freshly ground black pepper
3 T. dry sherry, optional

In a large, heavy frying pan or saucepan, melt butter and add vegetables. Sprinkle lemon juice over, cover tightly, and steam for about 10 minutes or until tender. Add beef stock, bring to a boil and simmer for about 10 minutes longer, or until well-flavored. Taste and add salt and pepper if necessary. Serve hot, adding sherry just before serving, if desired.

ENGLISH VEGETABLE SOUP
Yield: 4 servings

2 cloves garlic, minced
1 c. sliced carrots
⅓ c. sliced parsnips
½ c. chopped onion
2 T. butter or margarine
2¾ c. beef stock or broth
6 black peppercorns
2 bay leaves
6 sprigs parsley
1 sprig thyme *or* ⅛ t. dry
½ c. non-instant powdered milk
½ c. milk
Salt
Freshly ground black pepper
Parsley
Yogurt (optional)

In a large frying pan or Dutch oven, cook vegetables gently in butter for about 4 minutes. Stir frequently. Add stock and peppercorns, bay leaves, parsley, and thyme. Cover and simmer about 20 minutes or until vegetables are tender. Discard peppercorns and bay leaves. Place mixture into a blender; purée thoroughly. Add milks and continue to blend until thoroughly mixed. Taste and correct seasonings. Serve hot with parsley or a spoonful of yogurt as garnishes.

CHEESEY VEGETABLE SOUP
Yield: 6 servings

1 c. scrubbed, chopped carrots
¾ c. chopped celery
1 c. chopped onion
1 c. chopped green pepper (deseeded)
2 T. butter or margarine
¼ c. old-fashioned rolled oats
4 c. chicken stock
1¾ c. milk
½ c. nonfat dry milk
1 c. grated aged cheddar cheese
Salt
Cayenne pepper
Parsley

Place first four vegetables and margarine in a large skillet or Dutch oven and cook, stirring frequently, for 15 minutes or until vegetables are softened and golden. Stir in oats and cook, stirring regularly, for about two minutes. Gradually stir in stock. Bring slowly to a boil and lower heat. Allow mixture to simmer, covered, about 15 minutes. Add milks and stir until smooth and heated (do not boil). Add cheese and heat through (again, do not boil). Serve hot, garnished with parsley, if desired.

LETTUCE SOUP
Yield: 6-8 servings

½ c. chopped onion
2 T. butter or margarine
1 large head leaf lettuce or romaine, chopped
1 small bunch watercress, finely chopped
1 T. dill, tarragon, or chervil, chopped
6-7 c. chicken stock
Salt
Freshly ground black pepper
½ c. yogurt
1 egg yolk, beaten

Cook onion in butter until tender; add lettuce, watercress, and herb. Stir thoroughly, then cover and let steam over medium heat for about 5 minutes, stirring regularly. Do not brown lettuce. Add stock and let simmer 15 to 20 minutes. Taste and add salt and pepper as desired. Beat yogurt and egg yolk together; beat a little soup into yogurt mixture, then add mixture to remaining soup. Heat thoroughly but do not let boil. Taste and correct seasonings. Serve hot, garnished with watercress or the herb used in the soup.

ONION SOUP
Yield: 6-8 servings

3 T. butter or margarine
1 T. vegetable oil
5 c. onion, chopped
Freshly ground black pepper
2 T. whole wheat flour
7 c. beef broth (or, if broth is especially rich, part broth and part water)
1 bay leaf
4-6 slices whole wheat toast
1 c. grated Swiss cheese
Grated Parmesan cheese

Melt butter in Dutch oven or soup kettle. Add oil, onion and pepper to taste. Cover and simmer 30 minutes until onions are lightly browned. Sprinkle in flour; cook two minutes, stirring constantly. Add broth and bay leaf. Stirring well, bring just to boiling, cover and simmer 30 minutes or until onion is tender. Discard bay leaf. Correct seasonings. At this point, refrigerate for later use, serve as is, continue as following: Preheat oven to 325°. Pour soup into an ovenproof dish. (If it has been refrigerated, reheat.) Place toast on top, sprinkle with Swiss cheese and Parmesan cheese. Bake for 20 minutes; then broil until cheese turns golden. Serve immediately.

PISTOU
Yield: 8 servings

6 c. vegetable cooking juices or water
1 c. dried great northern beans, rinsed and sorted
⅓ c. chopped basil
5 cloves garlic, minced
2 medium potatoes, scrubbed well and diced
1½ c. green beans
2 c. onion, sliced
2 T. vegetable oil
3 large tomatoes, chopped
1 large zucchini, scrubbed and chopped
2 t. salt
  Freshly ground black pepper
½ c. chopped parsley

In a large kettle, bring water or other liquid to a rolling boil. Add dried beans slowly so liquid does not stop boiling. As soon as all beans are in liquid, reduce heat immediately. Cover and simmer 1½ hours or until beans are tender but not mushy. Stir in basil, garlic, potatoes, and green beans. Simmer for 15 more minutes. Sauté onion in oil until transparent. Add to soup with the rest of the ingredients. Simmer, covered, until zucchini is just tender. Correct seasonings. Before serving, sprinkle top with parsley.

BORSCHT
Yield: Approximately 7 cups

2 c. diced beets
½ c. diced carrots
1 c. diced onion
1 clove garlic, minced
2 T. minced parsley
2 c. water
2 t. margarine
2 c. chicken or beef stock
1¼ c. shredded cabbage or collard leaves
2 t. cider vinegar
  Salt
  Freshly ground black pepper
  Sour cream or yogurt
  Cucumber, grated (optional)
  Fresh dill (optional)

Place first five vegetables and water into a large saucepan or soup kettle. Bring to a boil and gently simmer, covered, 20 to 25 minutes. Add margarine, stock, cabbage, and vinegar and simmer until vegetables are tender. Add salt and pepper to taste. Serve as is or put mixture into a blender and blend until smooth. Chill and serve garnished with a tablespoon of sour cream and cucumber or fresh dill, as desired.

CUCUMBER SOUP
Yield: 4-6 servings

2 medium-size cucumbers
2 T. butter
2 c. chicken broth
  Salt
  Freshly ground black pepper
½ c. milk
¼ c. non-instant powdered milk

Peel cucumbers if skin has been covered with paraffin or is especially thick or bitter. Slice them in half lengthwise and scoop out any seeds that appear hard. Chop the cucumber slices. In a large skillet or saucepan, melt the butter over medium heat. Add the cucumber; stir, cover, and cook until cucumber is tender and transparent, about 10 to 15 minutes. Add broth, stir well, and season to taste. Let cool, add milk and powdered milk, and place mixture into blender. At medium speed, blend soup until smooth. Chill until ready to serve or heat very slowly and serve hot. Garnish with chives, parsley, or bits of raw cucumber.

CUCUMBER-YOGURT SOUP

For a variation of the above soup, after adding broth and allowing mixture to cool, stir in ½ cup (more or less, to taste) plain yogurt. Chill and garnish before serving.

"LEFTOVER" BEEF STEW
Yield: 4 or more servings

Leftover pot roast or other pieces of beef and bones
Meat juices (skim off hardened fat)
1½ c. canned tomatoes and juice
Leftover stew vegetables (onions, carrots, potatoes, etc.)
Other vegetables (green beans, cabbage, celery, etc.)
Beef stock or vegetable cooking water, if necessary
½ c. red wine, if necessary
Fried bacon, if necessary
Salt
Freshly ground black pepper
Parsley

Cut leftover meat into bite-size pieces and place in large soup kettle along with meat juices, tomatoes, and leftover vegetables. If there is not enough liquid, add beef stock and/or wine. If there is not enough meat, add a few strips of fried bacon. Let mixture simmer until vegetables are tender. Add salt and pepper, as desired. Serve hot, garnished with parsley.

MEDITERRANEAN SOUP
Yield: 5½ quarts

- 1 T. vegetable oil
- 2 lbs. meaty beef shanks
- 1 c. chopped onion
- 3 cloves garlic, minced
- 4 c. water
- 3-4 c. canned tomatoes in juice
- 2 c. tomato sauce
- ¼ c. parsley, chopped
- 3 basil leaves, chopped *or* 1 t. dry
- 1 bay leaf
- 2 c. carrots, diced
- 2 c. celery, chopped
- 2 c. shell macaroni
- 2 c. fresh or frozen green beans
- 1 c. fresh or frozen peas
- 2 c. cooked kidney beans
  Salt
  Freshly ground black pepper
  Freshly grated Parmesan cheese

In a Dutch oven brown beef shank pieces on one side in oil; add onion and garlic and brown the other side of the meat. Add water, bring to boil and skim. Add tomatoes, tomato sauce, parsley, basil, and bay leaf. Bring to boil again; reduce heat, cover and simmer for 1¾ hours.

Add carrots and celery; cover and simmer for about 45 minutes or until meat begins to fall off the bone. Remove meat and bones from soup; discard bones and fat. Dice meat and return to soup, adding water if you wish a thinner soup. Heat to boiling; add uncooked macaroni, green beans, and peas. Lower heat and simmer, covered, 15 to 20 minutes or until macaroni is tender. Stir occasionally. Finally add kidney beans and salt and pepper to taste. When soup is thoroughly heated through, serve garnished with parsley. Pass Parmesan cheese. This soup can be frozen.

CREAM OF CAULIFLOWER SOUP
Yield: 6-8 servings

- 1 large cauliflower, trimmed and broken into florets
- 2 T. butter or margarine
- ¼ c. finely chopped onion
- 2 c. finely chopped celery
- 3-4 c. chicken stock (brought to the boiling point)
- 2 c. milk
- ½ c. non-instant powdered milk
  Freshly grated nutmeg
  Salt
  Freshly grated black pepper
- ½ c. (or more) grated cheddar cheese

Place cauliflower florets in a large, heavy bottomed pan; cover with about ¾ inch of milk (from the two cups). Simmer, covered, 10 to 12 minutes or until florets are tender. Reserve a third of the florets. Melt butter in a skillet, add onion and celery; and sauté vegetables, stirring regularly, until tender. Place two-thirds of the florets in the blender with the cooking liquid. Purée until smooth, adding more milk if necessary. Blend in the chicken stock until of desired consistency. Add the powdered milk and the regular milk; blend till smooth. Reheat along with the reserved florets, onion, and celery until soup is heated through; add nutmeg. Taste and correct seasonings as desired. Serve hot, garnished with grated cheese.

OLD-FASHIONED BEAN SOUP
Yield: 4-6 servings

- 6 c. water or vegetable cooking liquid
- 1 c. dried navy beans
- 8 oz. ham, cut into bite-size pieces
- 1 large bay leaf
- 6 peppercorns
- 4 whole cloves
- 1½ c. chopped carrots
- 1¼ c. chopped celery with tops
- 1 c. chopped onion
  Salt
  Freshly ground black pepper

In large soup kettle over high heat, bring water and beans to boil; cook for 2 minutes. Turn off heat, cover, and let stand for at least 1 hour. Stir in ham, bay leaf, peppercorns, and whole cloves. Bring to a boil; skim surface and simmer, covered, 1½ hours. Discard seasonings from soup. Add vegetables and cook ½ hour or until vegetables are tender. Taste and add salt and pepper as desired.

CREAM OF MUSHROOM SOUP
Yield: 4-6 servings

2 T. butter or margarine
1 c. chopped onion
2 c. cleaned and sliced mushrooms
1 c. beef stock
1 drop liquid hot pepper sauce
2 c. milk
½ c. non-instant powdered milk
 Freshly grated nutmeg
 Salt
 Freshly ground black pepper

In a large frying pan or Dutch oven, melt butter; add onion and cook until transparent. Reserve ½ cup mushrooms for garnishing. Add remaining mushrooms to onion. Cover and cook gently, stirring regularly, about 4 minutes. Stir in stock and hot pepper sauce; bring to a boil and simmer about 4 minutes more, or until mushrooms are tender. Pour mixture into blender and blend thoroughly. Add milks and continue to blend until thoroughly mixed. Add nutmeg and reserved mushrooms. Return to heat but do not boil. Taste and salt and pepper as desired. Serve hot.

SPINACH OR SWISS CHARD SOUP
Yield: 4-6 servings

10-12 oz. fresh spinach or chard, washed and drained
1 recipe Cream of Mushroom Soup

Steam spinach until just tender; chop as desired. Add to Cream of Mushroom Soup as you return the soup to the heat. Do not boil. Taste and correct seasonings. Serve hot.

EASY GAZPACHO (WITH GARNISHES)
Yield: 4 or more servings

2½ c. tomato juice
1 T. sherry
1 T. white vinegar
2 c. beet juice (optional)
 Salt
 Freshly ground black pepper

Mix together the tomato juice, sherry, vinegar and beet juice. Add salt and pepper to taste. When well blended, cover and chill. Place your choice of the listed garnishes in small dishes on a tray. If you plan to use bread cubes, brown in hot oil about 3 minutes, then drain. Serve chilled juice mixture in individual soup plates; garnish with parsley and chives, as desired. Guests will spoon further garnishes into their own soup plates.

GARNISHES

1 tomato, diced
1 green onion, diced
1 green pepper, diced
1 cucumber, diced
½ c. diced celery
½ c. crisp, crumbled bacon
½ c. chopped black olives
½ c. slivered, toasted almonds
1 c. whole wheat bread cubes
1 T. olive or vegetable oil
 Parsley
 Chives

MIXED BEAN SOUP
Yield: 6-8 servings

½ c. dried red kidney beans
½ c. dried pinto beans
½ c. dried black-eyed peas
½ c. dried lentils
2 T. olive or vegetable oil
1 large onion, sliced
3 cloves garlic, sliced
3 large stalks celery and leaves, chopped
3 large carrots, scrubbed and sliced
3 tomatoes, quartered (optional)
⅓ c. fresh parsley, chopped
¼ t. thyme, crumbled
 Salt
 Freshly ground black pepper
 Freshly grated Parmesan cheese

Rinse and pick over beans; place in a large pot. Cover amply with water and soak overnight (or for at least 8 hours). (Or to speed up process, put 4 cups water in a large kettle, bring water to a boil, add beans and boil for 2 minutes. Cover pan, remove from heat and let sit for two hours. Proceed with the recipe.)

Drain beans but save soaking liquid. In a very large, heavy skillet or Dutch oven, heat oil and cook onion in it until it becomes transparent. Add soaked beans and garlic, stirring well to coat in oil. Stir in the rest of the vegetables and the soaking liquid. (Add another cup of water or vegetable cooking juices if there is not enough liquid.) Sprinkle the parsley and the thyme on top.

Simmer, covered, very gently for 2 to 3 hours or until beans are just tender. If necessary, add more water during cooking, but not too much for this soup should be thick. Check seasoning and add salt and pepper to taste. Serve with grated Parmesan cheese and garnish with parsley, if desired.

Pictured opposite
5 Vegetable Nituke, p. 17

CREAM OF LEEK AND POTATO SOUP
Yield: About 7 cups

4½ c. leek, washed, trimmed, split, and thinly sliced (tops, too)
3 T. butter or margarine
1¾ c. potatoes, scrubbed and finely chopped
1 c. water
2½ c. chicken, beef, or other broth
1 c. non-instant powdered milk
Salt
Freshly ground black pepper
Toasted rye croutons
Caraway or dill seeds (optional)
Chives, chopped (optional)
Parsley, chopped (optional)

In a large pan, cook leeks in butter until soft. Add potatoes, water, and broth. Simmer until potatoes are tender. Pour mixture into blender container and blend until smooth. (You might have to do this in two steps if there is too much soup for your container.) Stir in powdered milk and blend until thoroughly mixed. If mixture is too thick, add milk or water until you reach a desired consistency. Return to pan; heat but do not boil. Add salt and pepper to taste. Garnish with croutons and your choice of the optional items above.

SHARON'S TOMATO SOUP
Yield: About 12 servings

4 T. butter
1¼ c. chopped onion
¾ c. diced carrots
1 t. minced garlic
8 large ripe tomatoes
1 T. tomato paste
1 t. salt
¼ t. sugar
5 sprigs parsley
3 sprigs thyme
1 bay leaf
4 c. chicken broth

Melt butter in a soup kettle; stir in onion, carrot, and garlic. Sauté over low heat until vegetables are soft and lightly colored. Stir in rest of ingredients except broth. Bring to a boil and simmer, covered, 20 minutes. Remove bay leaf. Put into blender, or, if you don't wish to have small bits of tomato skin in your soup, strain. The mixture can be frozen at this point. When ready to serve, dilute with 4 cups chicken broth. Correct seasonings. Heat and serve. Garnish with fresh dill, chives, or parsley.

CRANBERRY JUICE
Yield: 2½ cups

3 c. fresh cranberries (washed and picked over)
2 c. water
⅓ c. honey (or more, to taste)
½ c. orange juice or apple juice

In a medium-size pan, cook cranberries in the water until all the skins pop open (about 5 minutes). Strain. Bring juice to the boil again, add honey, cook for a minute or until well blended. Remove from heat and cool. Stir in orange juice and serve well chilled.

SEVEN VEGETABLE JUICE
Yield: 5½ cups

3½ c. fresh or canned tomatoes, chopped, seeded and peeled, if desired
½ c. chopped celery
¼ c. chopped onion
¼ c. chopped carrot
½ c. chopped green pepper (deseeded)
½ c. chopped cucumber (deseeded)
2 sprigs parsley
Salt
Freshly ground black pepper
Dill (optional)
Worcestershire sauce (optional)

Place tomatoes in blender and purée thoroughly. Slowly add other vegetables while blender is still running. If mixture is too thick, add more tomatoes or juice. When well blended, add salt and pepper to taste. Chill and serve garnished with dill or Worcestershire sauce, as desired.

TOMATO JUICE
Yield: 4-6 servings

10-12 ripe tomatoes, chopped
1 slice onion
1 stalk celery, chopped
¼ bay leaf, crumbled
3 sprigs parsley
Salt
¼ t. brown sugar

Place tomatoes, vegetables, parsley and bay leaf in a large saucepan. Cook over high heat, covered, until tomatoes are tender, stirring regularly. Put through sieve; add salt to taste and brown sugar. Serve thoroughly chilled.

Vegetables

GARDEN HARVEST CASSEROLE
Yield: 6 to 8 servings

1 c. sliced and unpeeled eggplant
1 c. thinly sliced carrots
1 c. sliced green beans
1 c. diced potatoes
2 medium tomatoes, quartered
1 small yellow squash, sliced
1 small zucchini, sliced
1 medium onion, sliced
½ c. chopped green pepper
½ c. chopped cabbage
3 cloves garlic, crushed
3 sprigs parsley, chopped
 Freshly ground black pepper
1 c. beef bouillon
⅓ c. vegetable oil
2 t. salt
¼ t. tarragon
½ bay leaf, crumbled

Mix vegetables together and place into a shallow baking dish (13 x 9 x 2 inch). Sprinkle parsley and grind pepper over all. At this point you can refrigerate until ready to bake. Preheat oven to 350°. Pour bouillon into a small saucepan; add oil, salt, tarragon, and bay leaf. Heat to boiling; correct seasonings. Pour over vegetables. Cover baking dish with aluminum foil; bake 1 to 1½ hours or until vegetables are just tender and are still colorful. Carefully stir vegetables occasionally; but to preserve color, don't lift cover off for very long.

Note: You can substitute other vegetables if they are in harvest and they appeal to you.

PUMPKIN PURÉE

1 pie pumpkin, peeled and cut into small pieces (remove seeds and strings)
 Enough water to steam the vegetable

Place pumpkin pieces over boiling water in a large pot. Steam until tender. Mash or sieve, keeping pulp as dry as possible. Use immediately or cool over cold water and freeze.

Note: Winter squash can also be used.

VEGETABLES ITALIANATE
Yield: 4 servings

1 T. olive oil
2 c. thinly sliced onion
1 c. thinly sliced potatoes
1 c. chopped carrots
2 large cloves garlic, minced
1 cucumber, peeled if necessary and sliced (or zucchini)
 2 large tomatoes (or more), quartered
 Wine vinegar
 Dry mustard
 Sweet basil, chopped
 Salt
 Freshly ground black pepper

Heat oil in a large frying pan over medium heat; cook onions in it for a few minutes. Add potatoes and continue cooking. Stir in carrots, garlic, cucumber, and tomatoes. Cover and simmer, adding more oil if necessary. Stir regularly. Cook for 15 minutes or until potatoes are just tender. Stir in small amounts of vinegar, mustard, basil, and seasonings. Taste and continue to stir in vinegar and seasonings until vegetables are doused to your liking.

5 VEGETABLE NITUKE
Sautéed Vegetables
Yield: 4 servings

1 stalk celery
2 carrots, scrubbed thoroughly
1 medium onion
¼ head cabbage
1 clove garlic, chopped fine
2 t. vegetable oil
1 t. soy sauce (more or less, to taste)

Slice the vegetables into "matchsticks." In a large skillet, heat oil; stir in all the vegetables. Stir-fry for five minutes; reduce heat, add a few drops of water if necessary, and cook 10 more minutes, stirring frequently. A minute or so before the time is up, stir in soy sauce. Vegetables should be crisp and tender and retain most of their color. Serve with cooked brown rice.

MUSHROOM RISOTTO
Yield: 4 servings

2 T. butter or margarine
1 c. chopped onion
8 oz. mushrooms, washed and dried and sliced
½ c. dry white wine
1½ c. brown rice
4 c. (approximately) stock
2 T. butter or margarine
¼ c. freshly grated Parmesan cheese
Salt
Freshly ground black pepper

In a large frying pan, melt butter and add onion. Sauté onion until transparent. Add mushrooms and wine, stir thoroughly and cook until liquid is absorbed. Remove mushrooms. Add rice to frying pan and stir until rice lightens slightly in color. Stir in one cupful of the stock. Cook over low heat until liquid is absorbed. Add another cupful; when it is absorbed continue to add liquid until rice is nearly tender. Add mushrooms and continue cooking until rice is tender and fluffy, about 45 minutes. Stir in remaining butter, Parmesan cheese, and season to taste. Let stand, covered, a few minutes before serving.

ZUCCHINI STUFFED TOMATOES
Yield: 8 servings

8 medium, ripe tomatoes
2 T. butter or margarine
1 large zucchini, chopped
½ lb. mushrooms, sliced
1 c. chopped onion
1 large clove garlic, minced
¾ t. salt
2 basil leaves, minced
Freshly ground black pepper
1 c. whole wheat garlic croutons (toasted)

Scoop out pulp from the inside of each tomato, making certain not to cut a hole in the shell which should be about ¼ inch thick. Chop the tomato pulp. Preheat oven to 350°. In a large frying pan over medium heat, melt butter. Add chopped pulp, zucchini, mushrooms, onions, garlic, salt, basil, and pepper. Lower heat, stir frequently, and simmer until most of the liquid has evaporated (12 to 15 minutes). Stir in croutons. Immediately, spoon crouton mixture into tomato shells. Place stuffed tomatoes in large flat baking dish. Bake for about 20 minutes or until tomatoes are tender.

JACKIE'S FRIED GREEN TOMATOES
Yield: 4 servings

5 strips bacon
Vegetable oil
3 large green tomatoes, sliced ¼" thick
⅓ c. whole wheat flour or cornmeal
1 T. minced chives
2-3 basil leaves, minced
¼ t. salt
Freshly ground black pepper

Brown bacon strips, remove and drain, and reserve for another purpose (or use to garnish tomato slices, if you like). Dip tomato slices in flour to which has been added the chives, basil, and seasonings. Fry tomato slices in bacon fat (if there is not enough fat, add some vegetable oil). Have enough oil in the skillet so sides of the tomatoes are covered, but not the tops. Brown on both sides until tomatoes are tender. Drain on paper towels and serve immediately.

EGGPLANT PARMESAN
Yield: 8 servings

1 large eggplant, sliced into ¼"-slices
¼ c. dry whole wheat bread crumbs
¼ c. freshly grated Parmesan cheese
½ t. salt
Freshly ground black pepper
2 eggs, beaten
2 T. olive or vegetable oil
8 or more thin slices Mozzarella cheese
2 c. tomato sauce
1 large clove garlic, minced
1 t. oregano (if needed in tomato sauce)
¼ c. freshly grated Parmesan cheese
2 T. minced parsley

Mix crumbs, Parmesan cheese, salt, and pepper together in a flat dish. Place beaten eggs in a similar flat dish. Dip eggplant slices first in the egg mixture, then in the crumb mixture and brown on both sides in hot oil in a very large frying pan. Preheat oven to 350°. When all slices are browned, place in a large greased baking dish. Place a slice of Mozzarella cheese on top of each eggplant slice. Mix tomato sauce with garlic and oregano and pour over eggplant slices. Sprinkle Parmesan cheese on top. (You can refrigerate dish at this point if you wish to bake it later.) Bake 25 to 30 minutes or until eggplant is tender and sauce is bubbly. (Time will be longer if dish has been refrigerated.) Serve hot, garnished with a dusting of parsley.

Pictured opposite
Falafel in Pita, p. 33

EGGPLANT CASSEROLE
Yield: 6 to 8 servings

1 medium-size eggplant, thinly sliced
2-3 c. fresh Swiss chard or spinach, washed and drained
1-2 large tomatoes, thinly sliced
1 large sweet onion, thinly sliced
⅔ c. whole wheat bread crumbs (or part raw wheat germ)
Butter or margarine

Preheat oven to 350°. Place half of the eggplant slices in bottom of a buttered, 2-quart casserole. Place chard on top of eggplant; cover with the rest of the eggplant and pack down. Next place on the tomatoes, and on top, the onion slices. Pour white sauce over the vegetables; sprinkle cheese on top. Finally sprinkle on bread crumbs and dot with a little butter or margarine. Bake for 40 minutes or until eggplant is tender.

SAUCE

2 T. butter
2 T. whole wheat flour
1½ c. milk
Freshly grated nutmeg
½ t. salt
Freshly ground black pepper
½ c. grated sharp cheddar cheese

Melt the butter over medium heat in a heavy-bottomed pan. Stir in flour, cook until flour and butter have thoroughly integrated. Add milk and continue to stir until sauce thickens. Add seasonings.

MEATLESS MOUSSAKA
Yield: 8 servings

2 large unpeeled eggplants, sliced ½" thick
Vegetable oil
⅔ c. freshly grated Parmesan cheese
Tomato Sauce
Filling

Brush eggplant slices with oil; brown quickly on both sides. Preheat oven to 375°. Using a very large casserole dish, layer the moussaka as follows: Tomato Sauce, Parmesan cheese, eggplant slices, Filling, Parmesan, eggplant, Parmesan, sauce, and Parmesan on top. Bake, uncovered, 45 to 50 minutes or until dish is hot and bubbling. Let stand 10 to 15 minutes before cutting into servings.

Note: If you like, grate Mozzarella or other cheese on top of the sauce and sprinkle Parmesan on top.

TOMATO SAUCE

2½ c. chopped onion
2 large cloves garlic, minced
2 T. olive or vegetable oil
4 c. chopped tomatoes
2 T. fresh parsley, minced
1 t. salt
Freshly ground black pepper
¼ t. rosemary (optional)
1 c. canned tomato sauce or purée

Cook onion and garlic in oil in large frying pan over medium heat until transparent. Add tomatoes, herbs, and seasonings but not tomato sauce. Cover and simmer 1 hour; stir in sauce and simmer 15 more minutes or until of desired consistency. Correct seasonings.

FILLING

1 lb. creamed small-curd cottage cheese
1 egg
1 t. nutritional yeast
2 T. freshly grated Parmesan cheese
⅛ t. rosemary, crumbled
¼ t. salt
Freshly ground black pepper

Mix together all ingredients. Refrigerate until needed.

SWEET 'N SOUR STUFFED COLLARD ROLLS
Yield: 12 servings

24 medium-size, tender collard leaves
1¼ lb. ground beef
2 T. onion, minced
1 c. cooked brown rice
1 t. nutritional yeast
1 T. raw wheat germ
1 t. salt
Freshly ground black pepper
2 c. tomato sauce
1 t. minced onion
2 T. cider vinegar
2 T. honey

Steam collard leaves over boiling water until pliable. Preheat oven to 350°. Mix together the beef, onion, rice, yeast, wheat germ, salt and pepper. Divide mixture among collard leaves; roll into bundles, tucking in sides as you roll leaves. Place into a 11½ x 7½ x 1½-inch shallow baking dish. In a saucepan, heat tomato sauce, onion, vinegar, and honey. Correct seasonings. Pour over collard rolls. Bake, covered, 45 minutes or until bundles are tender.

Note: You can, of course, substitute cabbage leaves — choose dark green, tender leaves if possible.

Seeds and Legumes

HOW TO COOK SOYBEANS

2 c. cooking soybeans, washed and
   picked over
4 c. water
½ c. or more vegetable cooking liquid or
   stock

One way to cook soybeans is to soak for at least 6 hours; preferably soak overnight in water. The next morning, drain soaking liquid, add vegetable cooking liquid, and bring to a boil. Add soybeans gradually so boiling does not stop; turn heat down, cover, and let simmer 3 to 5 hours or until tender. (Be careful pot doesn't boil over or liquid doesn't evaporate — you may need to add extra liquid.) Another way to cook soybeans is to soak them for about 2 hours in a container that can be placed in the freezer. Freeze until solid or longer. Bring the vegetable cooking water to the boil and drop the frozen soybean chunk into it. Cover and let simmer 2 to 4 hours or until tender as desired. Use in recipes as desired.

SOYBEAN CHILI
Yield: 6 to 8 servings

½ lb. salt pork, cubed
1 c. chopped onion
2 lb. ground beef
1 c. tomato sauce
2 c. canned tomatoes and juice
1 T. cumin (or more)
4 large cloves garlic
¼ t. cayenne
2 T. salt
⅓ c. chili powder (or more)
4 c. cooked soybeans, drained

In a very large frying pan or Dutch oven, heat the salt pork over low heat until the fat runs. Remove cracklings. Brown the onion and beef in the fat. When brown, stir in tomato sauce, tomatoes, cumin, garlic, cayenne, salt, and chili powder. Let boil again, turn down heat and simmer about ½ hour. Add the soybeans and continue to simmer an additional hour or longer. Correct seasonings. Garnish with chopped raw onions, if desired.

SOYBURGERS
Yield: 4 to 5 servings

2 c. cooked soybeans
1 medium onion
1 large carrot
1 celery stalk
½ t. tamari or soy sauce (to taste)

Preheat oven to 350°. Purée soybeans in a blender or put through grinder (or mash with a potato masher). Grind onion, carrot, and celery. Add tamari to taste. Form into patties and place on a greased baking sheet. Bake approximately 7 minutes, turn to the other side and bake about 7 minutes more or until brown. Serve with a sauce, with cheese and bean sprouts, or in a sandwich, as desired.

ITALIAN SOYBEANS
Yield: 4 servings

2 T. olive or vegetable oil
1 c. chopped onion
3 large cloves garlic, minced
1 c. favorite tomato sauce
½ t. salt
  Freshly ground black pepper
½ t. oregano
½ t. basil
1 bay leaf
¼ c. dry white wine
2 c. cooked soybeans, drained

Heat oil in a large frying pan over medium heat. Stir in onion and garlic; cook until onion is transparent. Stir in tomato sauce, seasonings and herbs, wine, and soybeans. Cover and simmer for about an hour or until sauce resembles chili sauce. Discard bay leaf. Correct seasonings. Serve over rice or whole wheat spaghetti and pass the Parmesan.

SWEET 'N' SOUR SOYBEANS
Yield: 6 servings

2 c. dry, cooking soybeans
2½ c. pineapple chunks, drained (reserve liquid)
¼ c. brown sugar
2 T. cornstarch
¼ c. cider vinegar
2½ T. soy sauce
¼ t. salt
1 green pepper, cut into thin strips
½ c. onion, thinly sliced
½ c. bamboo shoots
Tomato quarters, optional

Cover soybeans with water and let soak overnight. If liquid is not bitter, simmer the soybeans in it in a covered pan about 5 hours or until beans are tender, adding more liquid if necessary. Drain. Combine brown sugar and cornstarch. Stir in pineapple juice, vinegar, soy sauce, and salt. Pour mixture over drained soybeans; cook and stir over medium heat until sauce thickens. When sauce is thick and smooth, stir in pineapple, pepper, onion, and bamboo shoots. Cook for about 3 minutes or until vegetables are crispy and tender. Correct seasonings. Serve plain or over hot brown rice. Garnish with tomatoes, if desired.

CURRIED LENTILS
Yield: 4 to 6 servings

3 cloves garlic, minced
2 medium onions, chopped
3 T. vegetable oil
1 c. dried lentils (washed and drained)
3 c. vegetable cooking liquid, bouillon, or water
2 T. curry powder
Salt
Freshly ground black pepper

In a large skillet over medium heat, cook garlic and onions in oil until transparent. Stir in lentils, liquid, and curry powder. Bring to a boil, cover, cook for 2 minutes, and turn off heat. In about one hour, turn heat on so mixture can simmer, covered, until lentils are soft but not mushy (about 15 minutes, depending upon the lentils). Add more liquid if necessary, during cooking. Taste and correct seasonings (add salt and pepper as desired). Serve hot as a side dish or cold as a salad. Garnish with chopped raw onions and yogurt or sour cream, if desired.

POOR MAN'S CASSOULET
Yield: 10 to 12 servings

2 qts. boiling water
6 c. Great Northern beans
6 strips bacon
2 lbs. lamb necks (or another inexpensive lean lamb cut)
2 large cloves garlic, minced
1 c. sliced onion
¼ lb. salt pork
1 t. salt
Freshly ground black pepper
½ t. thyme
¼ c. minced parsley
1 bay leaf
6 T. tomato pureé
1 c. dry white wine
1 lb. leftover pork roast, cut into bite-size pieces plus cooking juices
1 or 2 Polish or smoked sausages, sliced into ½" pieces
1 c. dry whole wheat bread crumbs
⅓ c. chopped parsley

Drop beans into boiling water, making certain water does not stop boiling; cover, lower heat, and simmer 30 minutes. Brown bacon and let drain on paper towels. In bacon fat brown lamb necks (make certain there are no bone splinters) and set aside. Brown garlic and onion in the same pan; turn off heat. Pour a small amount of bean broth into pan and scrape juices into the broth. Pour into bean kettle. After the beans have cooked 30 minutes, add lamb, garlic, onion, salt pork, seasonings, herbs, pureé, and wine. Simmer, uncovered, for an hour longer or until beans are quite tender. Add more water if necessary. Remove lamb and cut meat from bones; discard bones and bay leaf. Slice salt pork. Drain bean broth and correct seasonings; skim any fat off.

Preheat oven to 375°. Using an 8-quart casserole (or two smaller ones), layer beans on the bottom. Then add a layer of pork roast pieces, then lamb, sausage, beans, salt pork, bacon, and so on, ending with beans and topped with sausage slices. Add any meat cooking juices you have, then the bean cooking juices until liquid comes just to the top of beans. Spread crumbs on top and bake, uncovered, about 1½ hours. As top "crusts" over, push down into cassoulet. If beans dry out too much, add more bean cooking liquid. Serve immediately.

Pictured opposite
Steak and Kidney Pie, p. 28

HOW TO SPROUT SEEDS AND BEANS

¼ c. sprouting soybeans, mung, flax, black radish, alfalfa seeds, etc.
1 c. lukewarm water
1 qt. jar
Nylon mesh or cheesecloth
Rubber band

Wash and sort seeds. Place them in the jar with the water. Cover top with mesh and fasten with the rubber band. Allow them to stand, undisturbed, for about 8 hours or until fully swollen. Gently pour off the liquid, rinse the seeds with cool water, and drain — disturbing the seeds very little. (You want the seeds moist but not wet.) Place jar on its side in a dark place. Rinse three times per day with cool water. When the first leaves appear, place the jar in sunlight. Sprouts such as soybean sprouts are fully grown in about 3 to 4 days. Use as soon as possible in soups, sauces, salads, chop suey, omelets, vegetable dishes, etc. Many people also like them raw in sandwiches.

SAUTÉED SPROUTS
Yield: 4 servings

2 T. onion, minced
1 T. vegetable oil
1 T. margarine or butter
1 lb. fresh sprouts, rinsed and drained thoroughly
Soy sauce (optional)

Heat oil and butter over medium high heat in a large frying pan. Stir in onion and sauté a minute or two. Add sprouts and stir lightly but thoroughly. Add liquid if necessary. Simmer, covered, 5 to 8 minutes or until sprouts are done to your liking. Season with soy sauce, if desired.

MOM'S OLD-FASHIONED BAKED BEANS
Yield: 8 servings

3 c. dried beans (Navy, Great Northern, Lima, etc.), washed and picked over
5 c. water (or more)
¼ lb. bacon or salt pork, sliced
⅓ c. chopped onion
3 T. old-fashioned molasses
1 T. brown sugar
3 T. catsup
1 t. salt
Freshly ground black pepper

Soak beans in water overnight and, next morning, bring to a boil. (If you don't have time to soak them, bring the water to the boil, drop beans in so water doesn't stop boiling, turn down heat and let them simmer, covered, until tender, 35 minutes or more.) Preheat oven to 300°. (Or use slow cooker.) Drain beans, reserving liquid. Place bacon slices in the bottom of bean pot or other casserole with a cover. Pour beans into bean pot. Stir the rest of the ingredients into the bean cooking liquid; taste and correct seasonings. Pour the hot cooking liquid over the beans. Cover and bake 5 to 6 hours or until beans are well-flavored and liquid is mostly absorbed. (If beans get too dry, add more water or stock.) Uncover beans the last hour of baking, if desired.

BLACK BEAN CASSEROLE
Yield: 6 servings

1 lb. black beans
1 meaty ham hock
1 c. chopped onion
3 bay leaves
4 large cloves garlic, minced
Salt
Freshly ground black pepper
Chopped onion

Rinse and pick over black beans; cover with water and let soak overnight in the refrigerator. The next day, heat beans to the boiling point in a large kettle; add ham hock, onion, bay leaves, and garlic. Turn down heat and simmer 2 to 3 hours, covered, or until beans are tender and meat falls from bone easily. Remove ham hock, cut meat off the bone; discard bone and bay leaves. Taste and correct seasonings. Add meat back to dish and heat until piping hot and well-flavored. Serve with brown rice, if desired, and garnish with chopped raw onion.

Main Dishes

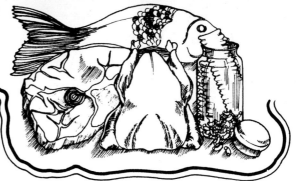

MOUSSAKA
Yield: 10-12 servings

3 lbs. eggplant, sliced ¼ inch thick
5 T. vegetable oil
2 T. butter or margarine
3 c. chopped onion
1 lb. ground beef
1 lb. ground lamb
¼ c. tomato paste
½ c. dry red wine
1 T. nutritional yeast
¼ c. raw wheat germ
⅔ c. parsley, chopped
¼ t. cinnamon
½ t. salt
   Freshly ground black pepper
1 c. freshly grated Parmesan cheese

Brown eggplant slices in hot oil in an electric frying pan or very large skillet. Keep warm (covered with foil) in a 300° oven. Add more oil as needed. When all slices are browned, melt butter in skillet; cook onion until transparent. Add lamb and beef and cook until meat is browned. Stir in the rest of ingredients except Parmesan cheese. Simmer, stirring frequently, until mixture is well cooked. Correct seasonings. In an 11 x 16-inch shallow casserole dish, layer eggplant, meat sauce, and Parmesan cheese, ending with eggplant. Pour Topping over. Either freeze for later use or bake, uncovered, in a 350° oven for about 1 hour or until top is browned.

TOPPING

8 T. margarine
8 T. whole wheat flour
4 c. milk
½ c. powdered milk
½ t. salt
4 eggs, well beaten
   Freshly ground nutmeg
2 c. cottage cheese or ricotta

Melt butter in a heavy pan; blend in flour and cook mixture, stirring constantly. Pour in milk, stirring constantly, until sauce is thick and smooth. Cool slightly, add the rest of ingredients. Correct seasonings.

VEAL PARMESAN
Yield: 4 servings

4 cubed veal steaks
1 egg
1 c. dry whole wheat bread crumbs
⅓ c. raw wheat germ
¼ c. grated Parmesan cheese
1 T. vegetable oil
4 thin slices mozzarella cheese
1 c. tomato sauce
   Parmesan cheese

Slightly beat egg in a flat dish. In another flat dish, mix together crumbs, wheat germ, and Parmesan cheese. Dip each cutlet into the egg first, then into the bread crumb mixture, making certain each piece is well covered. Preheat oven to 325°. In a large skillet, heat vegetable oil. Brown the breaded veal quickly on both sides and put into a large, flat baking dish. Cover each piece with a slice of mozzarella. Pour tomato sauce over and sprinkle additional Parmesan cheese on top. Bake for 45 minutes or until meat is tender and sauce is bubbly.

LIVER WITH WINE SAUCE
Yield: 4 servings

2-3 bacon strips
1 lb. liver, trimmed and sliced
¼ c. (or more) raw wheat germ mixed with
   2 T. whole wheat flour
1 c. onion slices
½ t. crushed thyme
1 t. salt
   Freshly ground black pepper
¼ c. dry red wine

Preheat oven to 350°. In a large skillet over medium heat, sauté bacon until barely browned. Remove bacon. Roll liver slices in wheat germ mixture and brown in bacon drippings. Grease a large flat baking dish; put liver in bottom. Spread rest of ingredients (except bacon) evenly over top. Place bacon strips over all. Bake for 15 to 20 minutes or until liver is done.

BAKED PORK CHOPS CREOLE
Yield: 4 servings

4 pork chops or steaks
2 T. vegetable oil
¾ c. uncooked brown rice
2 large ripe tomatoes, sliced into 8 rings
1 large onion, sliced into 4 rings
½ sweet green pepper, seeded and sliced into 4 rings
½ t. salt
  Freshly ground black pepper
  Pinch of thyme
  Pinch of marjoram or oregano, as desired
1½ c. chicken stock

Preheat oven to 350°. Brown pork chops on both sides in vegetable oil. Grease a flat baking dish lightly and pour rice into it. Place pork chops on the rice, and top each chop with the vegetable rings. Season with salt and pepper and desired herbs. Pour chicken stock over all. Bake, covered, for 1 hour or until rice is tender.

NALISTNIKI
(Meat Stuffed Crepes)
Yield: 16 crepes

CREPES

¾ c. sifted whole wheat flour
2 eggs
1¼ c. milk
1 T. melted butter or margarine

Put flour in medium-size mixing bowl, make a well in the center. Thoroughly mix wet ingredients together and pour into the well. With a wire whisk, stir ingredients together until nearly smooth. Let rest for about 15 minutes. Melt small amount of butter or margarine in a crepe pan over medium heat. When a drop of water sizzles, ladle 3 tablespoons of the batter into the crepe pan and move pan around until batter covers pan very evenly. Cook briefly until crepe will leave pan easily; turn over with spatula or fingers and cook briefly until lightly browned on the other side. Drain on toweling until ready to fill. Add more butter as necessary. Can be refrigerated at this point and heated later. Or bake immediately in a preheated 350° oven for about 15 minutes or until crepes are heated through and sauce is bubbly. Garnish with parsley if desired.

FILLING

¾ to 1 lb. cooked, leftover beef
2 hard-boiled eggs
1 medium onion
½ t. salt
⅛ t. dill seed
  Freshly ground black pepper
1 c. cottage cheese

Grind meat, eggs, then onion; stir in the rest of the ingredients and correct seasonings. Place part of mixture on each of the crepes, roll up, and arrange in a large, flat baking dish.

SAUCE

2 T. butter or margarine
2 T. whole wheat flour
½ c. milk
½ c. beef stock
  Salt
  Freshly ground black pepper
2 T. chopped parsley
2 T. chopped chives
1 c. cooked, sliced mushrooms

Melt butter in a small, heavy bottomed saucepan; stir in flour and cook for a minute or two. Slowly stir in milk and beef stock. Taste and add salt and pepper. As mixture thickens, add parsley and chives. Finally, when sauce is thickened and bubbly, add the mushrooms. Remove from heat and pour sauce over the crepes. Can be refrigerated at this point and heated later. Or bake immediately in a preheated 350° oven for about 15 minutes or until crepes are heated through and sauce is bubbly. Garnish with parsley if desired.

HI-PROTEIN LOAF
Yield: 6 servings

1 lb. ground beef
2 eggs
½ t. salt
  Freshly ground black pepper
1 medium onion, minced
⅓ c. soy flour
⅓ c. raw wheat germ
½ c. non-instant powdered milk
2 T. mayonnaise

Preheat oven to 325°. In a large bowl, mix ingredients together in order. Shape into a loaf and place in a lightly greased loaf pan. Bake for about an hour or until done.

STEAK AND KIDNEY PIE
Yield: 4-6 servings

3 oz. suet
1 large onion, sliced
1 lb. chuck steak, well trimmed and cubed
½ lb. lamb or beef kidney, well trimmed and cubed
1 c. beef broth
2 large carrots, sliced
3 T. chopped parsley
Salt
Freshly ground black pepper
1 t. Worcestershire sauce
¼ t. cayenne pepper
1 c. mushrooms, sliced vertically
1 T. whole wheat flour
½ c. cold water or leftover vegetable water
Egg yolk
Pastry for top of a 9-inch pie

Heat suet over medium heat in large skillet or Dutch oven. Add onion and sauté until translucent. Remove piece of suet. Add beef and kidney and brown lightly and quickly. Stir in beef broth, vegetables, except mushrooms, and seasonings. Cover tightly and simmer about two hours (until meat is tender), adding mushrooms the last 15 minutes. Preheat oven to 425°. Stir water into flour until well mixed. Pour into skillet with meat mixture and stir until sauce is thickened. Pour into 9-inch pie plate, place crust over meat, sealing edges tightly. Brush pastry with beaten egg yolk and make a hole in the center for steam to escape. Bake for 30 minutes or until crust is done. Serve immediately.

PASTRY
Yield: pastry for 9-inch pie

¾ c. butter or margarine
2 c. sifted whole wheat pastry flour
¼ t. salt
½ c. ice water

All ingredients should be cold. Mix flour and salt together in a medium-sized mixing bowl. With a pastry blender, blend in butter until mixture resembles crumbs. Add water all at once and stir until a ball of dough forms. Roll out ¼ inch thick on a floured cloth with a covered rolling pin, also lightly floured. Store in refrigerator, covered, until ready to put on top of pie.

YOGURT MEATBALLS
Yield: 4-5 servings

½ c. dry whole wheat bread crumbs
¼ c. milk
1 lb. ground beef
1 small onion, minced
1 t. salt
Freshly grated black pepper
1 egg
¼ c. raw wheat germ (or more)
1 T. vegetable oil

Soak bread in milk in a large bowl and mix in meat, onion, seasonings and egg. Beat thoroughly (with electric mixer if lightness is desired) until mixture is well blended. Shape into small meatballs, roll in wheat germ, and brown in heated oil in a large skillet over medium heat. Remove and drain balls when browned. When all meatballs are browned, put them back into the pan with a little broth or vegetable liquid if pan is dry and cover tightly. Simmer for 5 to 10 minutes or until done. Just before serving, pour yogurt sauce over.

YOGURT SAUCE

1 c. yogurt
1 T. lemon juice
Salt
Freshly ground black pepper
1 T. chopped parsley

Gently mix ingredients together and spoon over hot meatballs. Serve immediately.

QUICHE LORRAINE
Yield: 4 servings

½ lb. Swiss cheese, grated
2 T. whole wheat flour
¼ c. non-instant powdered milk
¼ t. salt
Freshly ground black pepper
1 T. onion, minced
3 eggs, beaten
1 c. milk
4-6 bacon strips, cooked and crumbled
1 unbaked 9-inch pie crust

Preheat oven to 325°. Combine grated cheese with flour, powdered milk, salt, and pepper. Scald milk in a heavy saucepan (150°). Gradually beat eggs and onion into milk. Add cheese mixture and stir until well blended. Sprinkle pie crust with most of the bacon bits. Pour cheese mixture into the pie crust and sprinkle the rest of the bacon in the center of the top. Bake for 30 to 40 minutes or until a table knife inserted in the center comes out clean.

SAUERBRATEN WITH GINGERSNAP GRAVY
Yield: 6 servings

3½ lb. chuck roast
1 t. salt
   Freshly ground black pepper
¾ c. red wine
1 c. cider vinegar
1 t. salt
6 whole allspice
1 c. chopped onion
1 c. chopped carrots
½ c. chopped celery
   Whole wheat flour
   Vegetable oil
8 gingersnaps, crumbled

Rub meat with salt and pepper and place in large glass bowl. Mix together the wine, vinegar, salt, and allspice. Pour over the meat. Add chopped vegetables. Cover bowl and refrigerate for 24 hours, turning meat 3 or 4 times. When ready to cook, take the meat from the marinade and roll in a small amount of flour. Brown on both sides in hot oil in a Dutch oven or large frying pan. Pour marinade mixture over the browned meat; heat to boiling, and then reduce heat to simmer, covered, for 3 hours or until meat is tender. To make gravy, strain marinade and cooked vegetables into a pan; stir in gingersnap crumbs and cook, stirring until mixture thickens. Serve with buttered whole wheat noodles.

RED AND WHITE CASSEROLE
Yield: 6-8 servings

8 oz. whole wheat noodles
1 T. butter or margarine
1 medium onion, sliced
1 lb. ground beef
2 c. canned tomatoes with juice
6 oz. tomato paste
1 t. crushed oregano
½ t. crushed basil
½ t. anise seed
1 clove garlic
1 c. cottage cheese
8 oz. cream cheese
½ c. thick yogurt or sour cream
1 T. chopped green pepper
1 T. chopped chives
1 T. melted butter or margarine

Cook noodles in boiling water until tender. Drain. Preheat oven to 350°. Cook onion in margarine in large skillet over medium heat for one minute, add beef and stir until browned. Put tomatoes, tomato paste, herbs, and garlic into blender and blend thoroughly. Pour over meat and stir until heated through. Combine cheeses, yogurt, chives, and green pepper. Mix thoroughly. Grease a 2-quart casserole; spread half the cooked noodles evenly over the bottom. Cover with cottage cheese mixture. Spread remaining noodles on top. Pour melted butter onto noodles and spread ground beef sauce mixture on top. Bake, covered, for ½ hour or until hot and bubbly.

CHICKEN POT PIE
Yield: 4 or more servings

1½ c. cooked chicken, diced
¼ c. chicken broth
½ c. cooked carrots, diced
½ c. cooked peas
2 T. fresh chopped parsley
2 T. butter or margarine
¼ c. chopped onion
¼ c. chopped celery
2 T. whole wheat flour
1 c. milk
2 T. non-instant powdered milk
2 T. wheat germ

Pastry for top of 9″ pie. Preheat oven to 400°. Mix chicken, broth, and vegetables together. In a heavy saucepan over medium heat, cook onion and celery in margarine until barely tender. Stir in flour and let cook for a few moments. Mix powdered milk with whole milk and stir into flour mixture. Add wheat germ and cook until sauce thickens. Gently stir chicken mixture into sauce and heat through. Pour into 9-inch pie pan and cover with crust. Slash crust a few times to allow steam to escape. Bake at 400° for 10 minutes. Lower heat to 325° and bake 30 more minutes or until done.

LARD PASTRY
Yield: 1 pastry for 9″ pie pan

All ingredients should be cold.

¾ c. whole wheat flour
½ t. salt
¼ c. wheat germ
¼ c. non-hydrogenated lard
1-1½ T. ice water

Mix dry ingredients together in a medium-size bowl. With pastry blender, mix in lard until mixture resembles crumbs. Add ice water and stir gently till mixture forms dough. Roll out dough to cover the top of a 9-inch pie pan and let stand in refrigerator, covered, until ready to use.

CHICKEN AND SPINACH CREPES
Yield: 6 servings

CREPES

2 eggs
⅔ c. whole wheat flour
¾ c. milk
1 T. vegetable oil

Combine ingredients in a large bowl and beat with a rotary beater until smooth. Cover and refrigerate for 1 hour. Grease crepe pan with waxed paper dipped in butter. Place pan over moderately high heat; when hot, spoon in about 2 tablespoons batter, tilting pan so batter covers bottom. Cook until the bottom of the crepe is lightly browned, turn and brown the other side lightly. Place crepes on paper towels until ready to use.

FILLING

1 lb. spinach (or chard), steamed and chopped
1½ c. cooked chicken breast
½ lb. fresh mushrooms, washed and chopped
2 T. butter
1 small onion, minced

Put chicken through coarse blade in meat grinder. In a medium-size frying pan, melt butter and add onion. Cook briefly and add mushrooms. Cook until mushrooms have given up their liquid. Cook and stir until all the liquid evaporates. Remove from heat. Stir spinach into mushroom mixture; add chicken. Stir in ½ cup of the Sauce, or enough to make the filling hold together.

SAUCE

5 T. butter
5 T. whole wheat flour
3 c. milk (or some half 'n half)
¼ t. nutmeg
Salt
Freshly ground black pepper
1½ c. grated Swiss cheese
⅓ c. freshly grated Parmesan cheese

In a medium-size, heavy bottomed pan, heat butter. Stir in flour, using a wire whisk. Let cook for about a minute. Add 2 cups milk, stirring rapidly. When thickened and smooth, stir in rest of milk and nutmeg. Add salt and pepper to taste.

ASSEMBLY

Preheat oven to 350°. Be certain you have mixed ½ cup sauce into filling. Stir Swiss cheese into sauce until smooth (over low heat if necessary). Spoon layer of sauce over bottom of large, flat, baking dish. Divide filling among crepes, and roll each crepe. Place crepes, seam side down, close together in baking dish. Spoon remaining sauce on top and sprinkle with Parmesan cheese. Bake 30 to 40 minutes or until thoroughly heated and lightly browned.

CHICKEN 'N BISCUITS
Yield: 4 servings

1½-2 c. cooked, diced chicken
½ c. diced cooked carrots
½ c. cooked peas
3 T. margarine or butter
¼ c. chopped onion
2 T. whole wheat flour
1 c. chicken broth
2 T. raw wheat germ
2 T. non-instant powdered milk
Salt
Freshly ground black pepper

Preheat oven to 400°. Gently stir together chicken, carrots, and peas. In a large skillet over medium heat, cook onion in margarine until translucent. Stir in flour and cook for a few moments. Stir in broth, wheat germ, and powdered milk. Cook until sauce thickens. Stir in chicken mixture gently; season to taste. Pour into 1½-quart casserole and drop biscuits on top. Bake for 10 minutes or until biscuits are done and chicken mixture is bubbly.

DROP BISCUITS

¾ c. whole wheat pastry flour
2 T. non-instant powdered milk
½ t. salt
2 t. baking powder
¼ c. raw wheat germ
2 T. vegetable oil
½ c. yogurt

Mix dry ingredients together in a large mixing bowl; make a well in the center and pour in oil and yogurt. Mix thoroughly and drop from a tablespoon on top of chicken mixture.

Pictured opposite
Chicken and Spinach Crepes

CHICKEN WITH YOGURT SAUCE
Yield: 4 or more servings

4 chicken breasts, split, *or* one whole fryer, cut-up
1 t. salt
1 t. paprika
  Freshly ground black pepper
3 T. whole wheat flour
2 T. butter heated with 2 T. vegetable oil
½ c. dry white wine
  Chicken broth, leftover vegetable water, or hot water
1 c. yogurt

Wash and pat dry chicken pieces. Mix together seasonings and flour in a paper bag. Drop chicken pieces in, one at a time, shaking the bag to cover the chicken evenly. Brown in a large skillet over medium heat in the butter mixture. Turn heat down when lightly browned and pour in wine. Add broth so that there is about ½ inch of moisture in the bottom of the skillet. Cover and simmer 45 minutes or until chicken is tender. Correct seasonings, push chicken to one side, and pour in yogurt. Stir very briefly. Put chicken pieces on a serving dish and spoon yogurt sauce over. Serve immediately.

CHICKEN CURRY
Yield: 4 servings

1 fryer, cut up *or* 4 chicken breasts
  Salt
  Freshly ground black pepper
¼ c. peanut or vegetable oil
1 green pepper, seeded and cut in strips
2 large cloves garlic, minced
1 c. chopped onion
1½ c. chicken broth
⅓ c. old-fashioned peanut butter
½ t. curry powder (or more, to taste)

Wash chicken pieces and pat dry with towels. Sprinkle with salt and pepper. Over medium heat, in a Dutch oven or large skillet, heat oil; stir in chicken pieces gently, browning on both sides. Push chicken to one side and add pepper, garlic and onion, stirring until onion is transparent. Stir in remaining ingredients and mix gently but thoroughly. When mixture starts to boil, turn heat down to low and cover. Simmer gently 30 to 40 minutes, turning chicken occasionally. When chicken is tender, correct seasonings, and serve with Peanut Pilaf.

PEANUT PILAF
Yield: 4 servings

2 T. vegetable oil
½ stick cinnamon
1 whole cardamom
2 whole cloves
½ c. raw peanuts
1 c. rinsed and picked-over brown rice
2 c. water
½ t. salt
⅓ c. yellow raisins
½ c. chopped dates (optional)

Heat oil in large frying pan; stir in cinnamon, cardamom, cloves, and peanuts. Sauté until peanuts are golden. Stir in brown rice and cook, stirring constantly, about 3 minutes. Add 1 cup water; bring mixture to a boil; add the second cup of water and salt. Again bring to a boil. Turn down heat, cover and let cook about 50 minutes or until rice is tender. (Make certain it doesn't scorch.) In the last few minutes of cooking, add the raisins and dates, if desired.

WHOLE WHEAT PIZZA
Yield: two 12-inch pizzas

1 c. lukewarm water
1 pkg. active dry yeast
1 c. unbleached flour
1 T. nutritional yeast
1 T. sifted soy flour
1 t. salt
1 T. oil
2 c. (approximately) whole wheat flour
  Filling as desired

Sprinkle yeast over water. Stir in 1 cup unbleached flour; mix in yeast, soy flour, salt, and oil. Stir in remaining flour until workable dough is formed. Knead until smooth and elastic (10 to 15 minutes). Place in lightly oiled mixing bowl; turn so all parts are oiled. Cover with a damp towel. Let rise in a warm place until more than doubled, 1½ to 2 hours. Punch down, cover with a towel, refrigerate until needed or until cold. Divide dough into two balls. On lightly floured surface with a floured rolling pin, roll balls into 12-inch circles. Place on well-greased baking sheets or pizza pans, turning edges of dough up slightly. Brush each circle with oil. Preheat oven to 425°. Fill as desired with your favorite tomato sauce, hamburger, Italian sausage, chopped green pepper, minced onion, anchovies, mushrooms, bacon bits, or whatever. Top with grated mozzarella, cheddar, or other desired cheese. Finally, sprinkle with Parmesan cheese. Bake 20 to 25 minutes or until crust is done.

FALAFEL IN PITA
(Deep fried chick-pea balls in pocket bread)
Yield: 2 dozen for appetizers, or use in pita

2 c. cooked chick-peas, well drained
1 c. onion
3 cloves garlic
½ c. parsley
½ t. baking powder
¼ c. raw wheat germ
1 t. ground cumin
1 t. ground coriander
½ t. salt
⅛ t. cayenne pepper
   Raw wheat germ
   Pita
   Shredded lettuce
   Chopped tomatoes
   Chopped cucumber

Put chick-peas, onion, garlic, and parsley through the fine blade of a grinder twice. Mix in baking powder, wheat germ, and seasonings. Pound the ingredients into a thick paste. (If your blender is strong enough, use it for this process.) Let stand 30 to 40 minutes. Form mixture into 1½-inch balls. Let stand 10 minutes; then roll in raw wheat germ until well coated. Heat oil in a deep fryer to 350° to 375°. Fry the falafel until they are a dark, rich golden brown. Serve as appetizers (can be dipped in Tahini Sauce) or use in pita. Slice warmed pita in half; put 2 falafel inside the pocket. Top with lettuce, tomato, and cucumber. Pour a small amount of Tahini Sauce on top. Garnish with parsley, if desired.

TAHINI SAUCE FOR FALAFEL
Yield: 1 cup sauce

½ c. tahini (ground, hulled sesame seeds)
3 cloves garlic, minced
½ t. salt
⅓ c. lemon juice
½ t. ground cumin
½ t. ground coriander
1 T. raw wheat germ
⅓ c. (about) chick-pea liquid
⅓ c. chopped parsley

Place all ingredients except chick-pea liquid and parsley into blender. Blend until smooth. Add liquid to desired consistency. Correct seasonings. Garnish with parsley. (Parsley can also be blended into sauce, if desired.)

SHARON'S FETTUCCINE SAUCE
Yield: 6 servings

1 c. chopped onion
2 cloves garlic, minced
3 T. chopped parsley
½ c. vegetable oil
6 unpeeled zucchini, diced
2 c. tomato sauce
2 t. minced sweet basil
1 bay leaf
½ lb. ground beef
   Salt
   Freshly ground black pepper
   Freshly ground Parmesan cheese

In a large skillet, sauté onion, garlic, and parsley in oil about 10 minutes. Stir in zucchini and simmer 5 minutes. Add tomato sauce, basil, and bay leaf and simmer 30 minutes. In a separate frying pan, brown ground beef and stir into tomato-zucchini mixture. Taste and add salt and pepper. Remove bay leaf. Serve over whole wheat fettuccine (ribbon noodles) with Parmesan cheese.

CHILI WITH BEANS
Yield: 8 servings

1 c. dried kidney or pinto beans
1 whole onion
3 T. vegetable oil
1 c. chopped onion
4 large cloves garlic, minced
2 lbs. ground beef
4 c. canned tomatoes with juice
¾ c. tomato paste
2 T. chili powder
1 t. crumbled sweet basil
1 t. crumbled oregano
1 t. salt
   Freshly ground black pepper

Soak beans in water to cover overnight. The next day, drain beans, put into a medium-sized pan with the whole onion, amply cover with water, and simmer, covered, for about two hours or until beans are tender. Add water if necessary during cooking. Taste and add salt as desired. Discard onion. In a large skillet over medium heat, cook the onions and garlic until golden. Stir in ground beef and cook until browned. Lower heat, stir in tomatoes, paste, and seasonings. Let mixture simmer for about an hour. Taste and correct seasonings. Stir beans into tomato mixture, cook a few minutes for flavors to blend, correct seasonings, and serve hot.

SALMON STUFFED CREPES
Yield: 8-10 servings

4 eggs
1½ c. whole wheat flour
½ c. unbleached flour
½ t. salt
　Vegetable oil
¼ c. Parmesan cheese

Mix together all ingredients except oil and ladle 2 to 3 tablespoons batter into a hot, lightly oiled crepe pan. Move pan around until batter covers pan evenly. Cook briefly until crepe will leave pan easily; turn over with spatula and cook until lightly browned on the other side. Drain on towelling until ready to fill. Add more oil as necessary. Divide the Filling among the crepes; roll up and arrange in a very large, flat baking dish (or two). Pour reserved sauce over and sprinkle with ¼ cup Parmesan cheese. You can refrigerate at this point or bake immediately in a preheated 375° oven for 15 to 20 minutes or until hot and bubbly. Garnish with a dusting of parsley.

SAUCE

½ c. vegetable oil
½ c. whole wheat flour
1 t. salt
　Freshly ground pepper
1 medium onion, minced
3 c. milk
1 c. cream
¼ c. dry sherry

Mix together oil, flour, salt, pepper, and onion in a large, heavy bottomed saucepan; cook over medium heat, stirring constantly until sauce is thick and bubbly. Slowly stir in milk and cream. When mixture again thickens, remove from heat, stir in sherry. Measure 3 cups of the sauce and set aside.

FILLING

1 c. Sauce
2 egg yolks, slightly beaten
1 lb. cooked salmon, drained, boned, and flaked

Blend small amount of remaining sauce into the egg yolks; return yolk mixture to saucepan, stirring constantly. Bring to a boil again, slowly, stirring constantly. Remove from heat; stir in the salmon.

COD AND MUSHROOM PARMESAN
Yield: 4 generous servings

2 lbs. cod fillets
1 lemon
1 c. white sauce
½ t. paprika
¼ t. nutmeg
½ c. freshly grated Parmesan cheese
¾ c. cooked, sliced mushrooms
½ c. parsley, minced

Preheat oven to 350°. Wash fillets in cold water, pat dry with paper towelling, and place in a large, shallow, greased baking dish. Sprinkle the juice of the lemon over the fillets. Add paprika and nutmeg to white sauce and correct seasonings. Add mushrooms to the sauce and pour sauce over fillets. Sprinkle cheese on top. Bake for 30 to 35 minutes or until done. Garnish with a dusting of parsley, if desired.

SOLE MEUNIÈRE AMANDINE
Yield: 4 servings

1 lb. sole fillets (fresh or frozen)
　Salt
　Freshly ground black pepper
　Whole wheat flour
¼ c. butter
½ c. chopped parsley
½ c. sliced almonds

Wash fillets and pat dry. Season with salt and pepper and dust lightly with flour. Melt butter in a large skillet over medium heat; add the fish and cook 2 to 3 minutes on each side. Don't overcook fish. Remove sole to large oven-proof serving dish and sprinkle with parsley. Sprinkle almonds evenly over the top. Put under broiler (not preheated) while you quickly stir the lemon juice with the pan scrapings. (If butter has cooked off, add a little more.) Remove fish from broiler when almonds are just browned and pour lemon sauce over. Serve immediately.

POOR MAN'S LOBSTER
Yield: 4 servings

1 lb. frozen haddock
　Lemon slices
　Butter, melted

Place the frozen fish into boiling water for about 5 minutes. Cut into 1-inch chunks (with electric knife if you have one). Broil for a few minutes until fish flakes easily with a fork. Garnish with lemon and dip in the melted butter.

Pictured opposite
Sharon's Fettucine Sauce, p. 33
Whole Wheat Noodles, p. 37

COD WITH VEGETABLES
Yield: 4-6 servings

1 lb. cod fillets, washed and patted dry
2 T. vegetable oil
2 large onions, thinly sliced
4 large garlic cloves, minced
3 carrots, thinly sliced
⅛ t. thyme
⅛ t. oregano
Salt
Tamari (or soy sauce)

Place cod in a large skillet and pour ½ cup water over. Cover and simmer for 5 minutes. Remove fish. In a separate skillet, heat oil and sauté onions, garlic, and carrots until onion is transparent. Pour fish cooking water over, add herbs, cover and simmer for 15 minutes. When carrots are barely tender, gently place fish on top of vegetables; heat through. Taste and season with a little salt and tamari, as desired. Serve with brown rice.

HELI'S HADDOCK WITH MORNAY SAUCE
Yield: 4 servings

1 c. sliced onion
2 T. butter or margarine
12 oz. spinach or chard, steamed and chopped
⅛ t. thyme
½ t. salt
Freshly ground black pepper
1 lb. haddock fillets, washed, patted dry, cut into halves
⅓ c. whole wheat flour
1 t. paprika
1 t. salt
¼ c. butter or margarine

Melt butter in a medium-size skillet; sauté onion until tender. Add spinach and thyme; stir. Cover and cook over low heat 7 to 8 minutes. Add ½ t. salt and pepper to taste. Place mixture in bottom of baking dish. Combine flour, paprika, and 1 t. salt in a paper bag. Drop fillets into bag; shake gently to completely flour. Sauté fillets in butter until golden; place on top of spinach. Pour Sauce over fish; sprinkle with paprika. You can set dish aside at this point to bake later. When ready to bake, preheat oven to 450°; bake 12 to 15 minutes or until thoroughly heated. Place under broiler 2 to 3 minutes until top is slightly browned. Garnish with parsley, if desired.

SAUCE

¼ c. butter or margarine
2 T. minced onion
¼ c. whole wheat flour
1½ c. milk
½ c. grated Parmesan or Swiss cheese
¾ t. salt
Freshly ground black pepper
¼ t. thyme

Melt margarine in a heavy pan; add onion and flour and cook, stirring constantly, about 1 minute. Slowly add milk, stirring to keep smooth. Over low heat, cook, stirring constantly, until sauce is thickened. Stir in cheese and seasonings. Taste and correct seasonings if necessary.

SALMON STUFFED EGGPLANT
Yield: 4 servings

2 good-sized eggplants
Salt
Vegetable oil
2 medium onions, chopped
½ c. cooked brown rice
1½ t. paprika
1 c. canned tomatoes
½ t. oregano
Pinch cayenne (or a few drops liquid hot pepper sauce)
1 7-oz. can salmon, bones removed and flaked
½ c. freshly grated Parmesan cheese
¼ c. melted butter or margarine

Cut eggplants into two lengthwise pieces. Score, sprinkle with salt, and leave, cut side down on a towel, for one-half hour. Preheat oven to 350°. Wipe eggplant dry, then brown cut surfaces in a small amount of hot oil in a large frying pan. Remove and place eggplant pieces on baking tin face down, and bake until tender, about 10 minutes. Cool. In a large skillet, heat 2 tablespoons vegetable oil and stir in onions. When transparent, stir in rice, paprika, tomatoes, oregano, and cayenne. Cook to a thick pulp, stirring occasionally. Scoop out pulp from the eggplant as carefully as possible, add to pulp, and continue to cook until well blended. Reserve skins for later use. Preheat oven to 400°. Add salmon to tomato mixture and stir in ¼ cup Parmesan cheese. Correct seasonings. Pile this mixture into eggplant skins, sprinkle with the rest of the cheese and melted butter. (Can be held for later cooking at this point.) Bake 10 to 20 minutes or until thoroughly heated and lightly browned. Garnish with parsley.

BROWN RICE SCRAMBLE
Yield: 8-10 servings

3 T. butter or margarine
2 c. brown rice
2 c. chopped onion
4 c. chicken broth or vegetable cooking
   water
4 large carrots, thinly sliced
4 large stalks celery, thinly sliced
   Leftover cooked seafood (salmon,
   smoked fish, etc.)
   Salt
   Freshly ground black pepper
½ c. chopped parsley

Melt butter in a very large skillet over medium heat. Stir in onion and rice, stirring constantly to coat rice thoroughly. When rice starts to brown slightly, pour in one cup chicken stock, turn the heat to low, and cover tightly. In about 5 minutes, stir in carrots and celery. Pour in more broth as necessary to prevent rice from sticking. Continue to cook for about 45 minutes or until rice is tender, adding more broth occasionally. The last few minutes of cooking, stir in leftover fish or what have you, season to taste, and sprinkle with parsley before serving.

NOODLES VERDE
Yield: About 8 ounces

1 c. whole wheat flour
½ t. salt
1 egg, beaten
¼ c. spinach, cooked and pressed dry
1 T. melted butter

Mix the flour and salt together in a medium-size mixing bowl. Combine the rest of the ingredients and stir into flour. Mix well. If dough is sticky, add a little more flour. Knead lightly on floured surface. Roll as thin as possible with a floured, covered rolling pin. Let stand 45 minutes. Cut into desired sized noodles. Put into tightly covered container to store. Cook in 2 quarts boiling water 8 to 10 minutes or until just tender. Drain.

WHOLE WHEAT NOODLES

Follow above recipe, leaving out spinach. You may need to use a little less flour.

WHOLE WHEAT NOODLES ALFREDO
Yield: 6 servings

1 lb. whole wheat noodles
½ c. lightly salted butter
2 c. Parmesan cheese, freshly grated
½ t. freshly ground white or black pepper

Cook noodles in salted, boiling water for about 8 minutes or until *al dente*. Drain and put into a hot serving dish. Pour remaining ingredients on top and toss lightly but thoroughly. Serve immediately.

PASTA MOUSSAKA
Yield: 4 servings

2 T. olive oil or vegetable oil
1 lb. ground beef or lamb
1 c. chopped onion
2 large cloves garlic, minced
2 c. canned tomatoes
½ t. salt
   Freshly ground black pepper
¼ t. brown sugar
1 bay leaf
   Pinch of rosemary or marjoram
   Pinch of oregano and sweet basil
1 c. white sauce
3 oz. grated Cheddar or similar cheese
6 oz. spinach or whole wheat lasagna
   noodles
1 green pepper, seeded and sliced
2 ripe tomatoes, sliced
¼ c. freshly grated Parmesan cheese

In a large frying pan, heat oil and stir in the meat, onion, and garlic. Cook until lightly browned. Add tomatoes, salt, pepper, sugar, and herbs. Cover and simmer for about 30 minutes or until sauce is well flavored. Taste and correct seasonings. Discard bay leaf. Stir grated Cheddar cheese into the white sauce and set aside for later assembly. Drop the lasagna into a large kettle containing boiling, salted water. Cook until tender; drain. Pour the meat sauce in the bottom of a shallow baking dish. Cover with lasagna noodles. Spoon a thin layer of cream sauce on top. Place green pepper and tomato slices on top. Cover the dish with the remaining cream sauce and sprinkle with Parmesan cheese. You can refrigerate dish at this point for later baking, or place it immediately in a preheated 350° oven for 15 to 20 minutes or until dish is thoroughly heated through and bubbly. You can place under broiler to brown the top a bit, if you like.

Breads and Breakfasts

WHOLE WHEAT PITA
Yield: About 16 "slices"

POCKET BREAD

- 2 pkg. dry yeast (½ oz.)
- 3 c. lukewarm water
- 3 T. honey
- 2 t. salt
- 3 c. unbleached flour
- 3-4 c. whole wheat flour
- Vegetable oil

Place yeast, ½ cup water, honey and salt in a small bowl and let stand in a warm place for 10 minutes. Place unbleached flour and 1 cup whole wheat flour in large mixing bowl. Add 2½ cups lukewarm water and the yeast mixture. Stir thoroughly with a wooden spoon for 1 minute and add 2 more cups whole wheat flour or enough to make a workable dough. Place on well-floured board and knead until smooth (about 10 to 15 minutes). Add more flour to board if necessary. Lightly grease a large mixing bowl with vegetable oil. Place dough in it, turn so all sides are greased. Cover with a damp towel and let stand in a warm place about one hour or until almost doubled in size.

Punch dough down and divide into approximately 16 balls. Flatten the dough into rounds about ¼ inch thick. Sprinkle lightly with flour and place the rounds on a floured cloth. Cover with another floured cloth and allow to rise again in a warm place.

Preheat oven to 475°. Lightly oil two large baking sheets and place in oven to heat for a few minutes while oven is heating. When the bread rounds have risen, slip them onto the hot baking sheets, sprinkle tops with cold water, and bake for 6 to 10 minutes. Do not open the oven door until you smell the baking bread (rather than the yeasty aroma). Remove rounds from baking sheets immediately after removing from the oven and place on wire racks to cool. You can freeze pita. If you wish to reheat, wrap in aluminum foil and heat in oven.

Pictured opposite
Old-Fashioned Whole Wheat Bread, p. 40
Sourdough Rye Bread, p. 41
Apple Bread, p. 44
Grandma Earle's Graham Muffins, p. 43
Whole Wheat Scones, p. 45

HI-PROTEIN BREAD
Yield: 2 loaves

- 2 pkgs. dry yeast
- 2 c. lukewarm water
- ¼ c. brown sugar
- ¼ c. old-fashioned molasses (unsulphured)
- 1 egg, beaten
- 4-5 c. whole wheat flour
- ¼ c. soy flour
- 1 c. non-instant powdered milk
- ¼ c. raw wheat germ
- 2 T. nutritional yeast
- 2 t. salt

Mix together the yeast, water, molasses and sugar in a large bowl and let stand in a warm place for five minutes. Mix in egg and 3½ cups flour. Beat thoroughly with electric mixer. In a separate bowl mix together the 5 remaining ingredients. Gradually stir the dry ingredients into the wet. Using a wooden spoon, stir in additional whole wheat flour until a soft dough is formed. Turn dough out onto a well-floured surface and knead until smooth (5 to 10 minutes). Place dough in a well-greased bowl, cover with a damp towel, and let rise in a warm place (85°) for about one hour or until dough doubles in volume. Punch down, let rest for 10 minutes, covered. Then divide the dough into two loaves and place in greased bread pans. Cover with damp towel and let rise in a warm place about 30 minutes or until doubled in volume. Preheat oven to 350°. Bake loaves about an hour or until done. Remove immediately from pans and brush top crust with butter.

Note: For a change, before adding the final flour, stir in sunflower seeds, sesame seeds, sun-dried raisins, and/or whatever nuts you would like to have in your bread.

OLD-FASHIONED WHOLE WHEAT BREAD
Yield: 2 loaves

Have all ingredients at room temperature, except water.

3 c. warm water (or potato water or light stock)
2 ⅝-oz. cakes yeast
7-8 c. whole wheat flour
½ c. honey
2 t. salt
¼ c. vegetable oil

In a very large mixing bowl combine water and yeast (smashed down with a fork); add 3 cups flour. Mix batter well, cover with a towel, and let stand 15 minutes. Add honey, salt, and oil; mix well. Gradually add 3 to 4 more cups flour. Mix thoroughly until soft dough forms which leaves the sides of the bowl. (A little more flour may be added if necessary.) On floured board, knead and stretch thoroughly with floured hands for 5 to 10 minutes. *Don't under knead.* Place in a large, well-greased bowl; turn to grease all sides and let rise until nearly doubled. Punch down, divide into two parts and form into loaves. Place in lightly greased, warmed tins. Cover with a damp towel and set in warm place (85°) to rise for one hour or until dough doubles its volume. Preheat oven to 450°. Immediately after putting bread in oven, reduce heat to 375°. Bake 35 to 45 minutes or until done. Remove from pans immediately and brush top crusts with butter. Let cool on wire racks.

FINNISH RYE BREAD
Yield: 2 loaves

2 pkgs. active dry yeast
¼ c. lukewarm water
¼ c. brown sugar, firmly packed
¼ c. old-fashioned molasses
2 t. salt
2 T. margarine
1½ c. hot water
2½ c. medium rye flour
3 T. caraway seeds
1 c. unbleached flour
2½ to 3 c. whole wheat flour

Sprinkle yeast on lukewarm water. Set aside. In a large bowl, stir together, brown sugar, molasses, salt, and margarine; add 1½ cups hot water and stir until sugar is dissolved. Cool to lukewarm. Stir in rye flour with a wooden spoon. Add yeast mix-ture and caraway seeds. Stir in unbleached flour. Finally stir in whole wheat flour until a workable dough forms. Turn out onto floured surface. Cover, let rest 10 minutes. Knead until smooth (about 10 minutes).

Place dough in lightly greased bowl, turn once to grease surface. Cover and let rise in warm place till double (1½ to 2 hours). Punch down. Divide into two sections and form dough into two balls. Cover and let rest 10 minutes. Place round loaves on well-greased baking sheet. Cover and let rise until almost doubled in a warm place. Preheat oven to 375°. Bake 25 to 30 minutes or until done. Butter tops if you wish a soft top crust. Let cool on wire racks.

100% WHOLE WHEAT REFRIGERATOR BREAD
Yield: 2 loaves

6-7 c. whole wheat flour
2 pkgs. dry yeast
2 t. salt
⅓ c. honey
3 T. margarine (room temperature)
2½ c. very hot water
Vegetable oil

In a large mixing bowl, stir together 2 cups of the flour, dry yeast, and salt. Add honey and margarine. Pour in hot water all at once and beat with electric mixer for two minutes at medium speed. Add 1½ cups more flour and continue beating with electric mixer until thick and elastic (about one minute). With a wooden spoon, stir in two more cups of the remaining flour. Gradually add more flour until a soft dough is formed. Turn out onto lightly floured board. Knead 5 to 10 minutes with floured hands or until dough is smooth. Cover with a towel and let rest for 20 minutes. Punch down and divide in two. Shape into smooth loaves and place in well greased bread pans.

Brush surface of dough with oil; cover pans with a towel and refrigerate.

You can bake the bread after two hours, 5 to 6 hours is, in my opinion, even better. Do bake it within 24 hours.

Preheat oven to 400°. Take bread out of refrigerator and let stand uncovered for 10 minutes while oven is heating. Bake for 35 to 45 minutes or until done.

Remove from pans immediately. Brush tops with butter.

SOURDOUGH STARTER

If you aren't already familiar with sour dough, you're in for a real treat. It's amazingly easy to work with and very versatile. Since most of our houses are so cool in winter, you might find it is easier to get your starter going in summer. Or try to locate a warm spot in your house — near the back of your refrigerator, for example. Or you can "incubate" in the oven — just put a pan of very hot water on the lower shelf and your starter on the top shelf. Do keep your starter out of drafts.

STARTER

2 c. lukewarm water
1 pkg. active dry yeast
½ c. unbleached flour
½ c. whole wheat flour
1 c. rye flour

Place water in a glass mixing bowl, sprinkle with yeast. Stir with a wooden spoon until yeast is dissolved. Add flour and beat until smooth. (You can substitute flours, if you wish; have fun experimenting.) Cover with a towel; let stand in warm place (80°-85°) for 48 hours. Stir once or twice a day with a wooden spoon. After removing what you need for your recipe, stir equal amounts of flour and water (for example, 1 cup flour and 1 cup lukewarm water) into the starter. Let "ferment" about 5 hours at room temperature, then cover and refrigerate in a wide-mouthed glass container. (Don't put cover on tightly; the jar might crack during fermentation.) Used regularly and replenished (about once a week), sourdough starter can be kept indefinitely. Wash out the glass container regularly. "Separation" of the starter is normal; just stir with a wooden spoon thoroughly before using.

Note: Always have starter at room temperature before using in recipe.

SOURDOUGH RYE BREAD
Yield: 2 loaves

You must plan ahead to make this bread if you don't have a starter, but the final results are well worth it!

1 pkg. active dry yeast
1¼ c. lukewarm water
3 T. molasses or sorghum
2 t. salt
1½ c. starter (at room temperature)
1 T. caraway seed (or more, if desired)
2 c. rye flour
4 c. (approximately) whole wheat flour

Pour water into a large mixing bowl; sprinkle with the yeast. Stir in next four ingredients and finally add flour. Mix thoroughly. Dough will be soft. Cover with a cloth and let stand in a warm place for an hour or until doubled in bulk. Turn dough out on heavily floured surface and knead until smooth (about 10 minutes). Shape into two round loaves and set onto greased baking sheets (sprinkled with cornmeal, if desired), or form them into loaves and place them into two greased bread tins. Cover and allow to rise in a warm place 45 minutes or until almost doubled.

Preheat oven to 400°. Brush loaves with slightly beaten egg, if desired. Place loaves into oven and bake 30 to 35 minutes or until done. Remove bread from tins to cool.

SOURDOUGH WHOLE WHEAT BREAD
Yield: 2 loaves

Use 100% whole wheat flour in the above recipe and leave out the caraway seeds. You might wish to use honey instead of molasses if you wish a lighter flavored bread. You can stir in ¼ cup soy flour if you wish added protein. You can also stir in raisins, nuts, seeds, or whatever appeals to you. If you wish a "higher" loaf, substitute unbleached flour for some of the whole wheat.

"FRENCH" BREAD
Yield: 2 loaves

Following suggestions under whole wheat bread, shape dough into 2 long loaves. Place on greased baking sheets. When raised, bake on top shelf of oven with a large cake pan filled with hot water on the bottom shelf of the oven. Bake 20 to 25 minutes or until done.

SOURDOUGH BISCUITS
Yield: 12 biscuits

1 c. starter, at room temperature
1 c. whole wheat flour
1 t. baking soda
1 T. baking powder
1 t. salt
1 t. nutritional yeast
¼ c. vegetable oil

Preheat oven to 425°. Sift together the flour, soda, baking powder, salt, and nutritional yeast. Stir the dry ingredients into the starter; then add the oil. Stir until mass of dough is formed. Turn dough out onto lightly floured board and knead a few times. Roll with a lightly floured rolling pin till dough is ½ inch thick. Cut with a lightly floured, round biscuit cutter. Place on a lightly greased baking sheet and bake 8 to 10 minutes or until lightly browned. Serve hot.

GRANDMA EARLE'S GRAHAM MUFFINS
Yield: 12-18 muffins

1¾ c. whole wheat pastry flour
¼ c. wheat germ
¼ c. non-instant powdered milk
½ c. brown sugar
1½ t. salt
2½ t. baking powder
½ c. vegetable oil
1 egg, beaten
1 c. yogurt (or sour milk)

Preheat oven to 400°. Mix together dry ingredients in a large mixing bowl. Make a well in the center and stir in oil, egg, and yogurt until all dry ingredients are just wet. Pour into muffin cups or lightly greased muffin tins and bake 20 to 25 minutes or until done.

OATMEAL MUFFINS
Yield: 12-16 muffins

1 c. whole wheat pastry flour
¼ c. brown sugar
¼ c. raw wheat germ
¼ c. non-instant milk powder
½ t. salt
1 T. baking powder
3 T. margarine or butter
1 c. rolled oats
1 egg, beaten
1 c. milk
½ c. raisins, optional

Preheat oven to 425°. Mix together the first six ingredients in a large mixing bowl. Cut in margarine with a pastry blender until mixture resembles crumbs. Add oatmeal and blend. Add eggs and milk, stirring lightly. Pour into muffin cups or lightly greased muffin tins and bake 15 minutes or until done.

BANANA-NUT BREAD
Yield: 1 loaf

¾ c. honey
¼ c. vegetable oil
3 mashed, ripe bananas
2 eggs
¼ t. salt
2 c. whole wheat flour
2½ t. baking powder
¼ c. wheat germ
¼ c. non-instant powdered milk
¼ c. broken nuts

Preheat oven to 325°. Stir together first four ingredients. Separately stir together dry ingredients, except nuts, and combine with wet ingredients. Blend thoroughly. Stir in nuts and pour into greased bread pan. Bake about an hour or until top springs back when touched lightly.

ZUCCHINI BREAD
Yield: 3 loaves

3 eggs
1½ c. brown sugar, firmly packed
1 c. vegetable oil
1 t. salt
1 t. baking soda
¼ t. baking powder
1 t. cinnamon
1 t. vanilla
3 c. whole wheat flour
¼ c. soy flour
3 c. zucchini, scrubbed, grated, and well drained
¾ c. chopped walnuts or raw sunflower seeds
¾ c. raisins

Preheat oven to 350°. In a large mixing bowl, beat eggs until foamy. Add sugar and oil and beat thoroughly. Stir in salt, soda, baking powder, cinnamon, and vanilla. Add flours alternately with zucchini. Stir in nuts and raisins. Grease and flour lightly 3 loaf pans (8½ x 4½ x 2⅝) or 2 larger or 4 smaller. Bake one hour or until done.

43

PUMPKIN BREAD
Yield: 3 loaves

¾ c. margarine or shortening
2¼ c. brown sugar, firmly packed
4 eggs
2 c. cooked pumpkin purée
⅔ c. water
3¾ c. whole wheat flour
1 T. nutritional yeast
2 T. soy flour
½ t. baking powder
2 t. baking soda
1 t. salt
1¼ t. cinnamon
1¼ t. ground cloves
⅔ c. regular or golden raisins or chopped dates
⅔ c. chopped nuts

Preheat oven to 350°. In a large mixing bowl, cream shortening and sugar thoroughly; add eggs and beat until light. Stir in pumpkin and water. In a separate bowl, stir together the flour, nutritional yeast, soy flour, baking powder, soda, salt, and spices. Stir dry ingredients into pumpkin mixture. Finally fold in nuts and raisins. Pour into 3 well-greased 9 x 5 x 3-inch loaf pans or 1-pound coffee cans. Bake for 1 hour or until done (toothpick inserted in center comes out clean). Let cool 10 minutes before removing from pans to finish cooling on wire racks. Tastes better the second day.

CRANBERRY-ORANGE BREAD
Yield: 1 loaf

1¾ c. whole wheat flour
¼ c. wheat germ
2 T. soy flour
¾ c. brown sugar
1½ t. baking powder
½ t. baking soda
2 T. margarine, melted and cooled slightly
  Grated rind and juice of 1 orange plus water or more orange juice to make ¾ c.
1 egg, beaten
1 c. raw cranberries, cut in halves

Preheat oven to 350°. In a large bowl, blend dry ingredients. Mix in margarine, orange mixture, and egg. Fold in cranberries. Pour into well-greased 9 x 5 x 3-inch loaf pan. Bake 45 to 60 minutes or until top springs back when touched lightly and bread pulls away slightly from sides of pan. Cool about 10 minutes before removing from pan. Cool on wire rack. (Bread is better the second day.)

APPLE BREAD
Yield: 1 loaf

½ c. margarine
½ c. honey
¼ c. old-fashioned molasses
2 eggs
2 t. baking powder
½ t. salt
1⅔ c. whole wheat flour
⅓ c. non-instant powdered milk
⅔ c. raw wheat germ
2 c. chopped, peeled apples
⅔ c. broken nuts

TOPPING

4 T. melted margarine
5 T. whole wheat flour
1 T. wheat germ
4 T. brown sugar, well packed
2 t. cinnamon

Preheat oven to 350°. Mix together thoroughly the first four ingredients. Stir dry ingredients together and combine with wet, blending well. Stir in apples until well blended and add nuts. Pour into well-greased bread pan. Mix topping together with a fork and sprinkle evenly over batter. Bake for one hour or until top springs back when pressed lightly.

JULIA'S MINCEMEAT BREAD RING
Yield: 1 loaf

1½ c. whole wheat flour
¼ c. raw wheat germ
2 T. soy flour
1 T. baking powder
2 t. nutritional yeast
1 t. allspice
½ t. salt
1 c. green tomato (or other) mincemeat
¼ c. milk
2 eggs, well beaten
½ c. brown sugar, firmly packed
3 T. vegetable oil
½ c. chopped nuts

Preheat oven to 350°. Mix together first 7 ingredients. In separate bowl, combine mincemeat, milk, eggs, brown sugar, oil, and nuts. Add flour mixture and stir until just blended. Pour into greased 8-inch ring mold. (Other molds can be used; baking times will differ.) Bake for one hour or until pick inserted comes out clean and bread pulls back slightly from side of pan. Cool 10 minutes. Remove from pan and cool thoroughly.

SOURDOUGH PANCAKES
Yield: About 30 silver dollar
sized cakes

1 c. sourdough starter
2 c. whole wheat flour
2 c. lukewarm milk
1 t. salt
2 t. baking soda dissolved in ¼ c. milk
2 eggs
3 T. vegetable oil
2 T. honey

Approximately 12 hours before making the pancakes (the night before) mix starter with flour, milk, and salt in a glass bowl. Cover with a towel and let stand in a warm place. When you are ready to make the pancakes, stir in the remaining ingredients; mix well. If you desire thinner pancakes, stir in more milk. Bake on a lightly greased, hot griddle.

SOURDOUGH WAFFLES
Yield: About 10 waffles

Follow the sourdough pancake recipe; increase vegetable oil to 5 tablespoons. Bake on hot, lightly greased waffle iron or according to manufacturer's instructions.

QUICK OVEN "PANCAKE"
Yield: 2 or more servings

2 T. butter or margarine
¼ c. whole wheat flour
¼ c. unbleached flour
½ c. milk (at room temperature)
2 well-beaten eggs (at room temperature)

Preheat oven to 425°. Place margarine in a 9-inch iron skillet or comparable oven-proof dish or pan, and melt the margarine. Place flours in a medium-sized mixing bowl; make a well in the center and pour in milk. Beat eggs into the batter. Don't break up lumps. Pour mixture into skillet with the melted margarine and place into oven immediately. Bake for 15 minutes or until lightly browned and puffed up. Serve hot with crushed fruit, maple syrup, or other favorite topping.

WHOLE WHEAT SCONES
Yield: 14-16 scones

2 c. whole wheat flour
2 T. brown sugar
2 t. baking powder
¼ t. salt
1 T. butter
1 egg
½ c. currants or raisins
¾ c. yogurt (more or less)

Preheat oven to 450°. Mix together dry ingredients; blend in butter with a pastry blender until mixture resembles crumbs. Mix in the egg and currants. Stir in yogurt gadually until a thick dough is formed. Knead lightly on floured cloth. Roll out to ¾-inch thickness. Cut with a round cutter and place on a greased baking tin. Brush tops with milk or egg. Bake for 10 to 15 minutes or until done.

CRUNCHY GRANOLA
Yield: 9 cups

4 c. rolled oats or a mixture of grains
2 c. whole wheat flour
1 c. raw wheat germ
1 c. bran
1 c. soy flour
1 T. nutritional yeast
2 t. salt
⅓ c. hot water
½ c. honey
1 c. vegetable oil
1 c. chopped nuts

Preheat oven to 275°. In a large bowl, mix together the dry ingredients (except nuts). Mix oil, honey, and water together and stir into dry ingredients. Stir until mixture resembles crumbs. Add nuts. Spread mixture very thinly onto two very large baking sheets. Occasionally turn mixture so it bakes evenly. Bake about 1 hour or until crisp and golden. Cool and store in a large container with a tightly fitting cover. Eat as a cereal with milk, fruit, nuts, or yogurt added.

MUESLI
Yield: About 2 quarts

1 lb. rolled or flaked wheat
1 lb. rolled oats
1 lb. rolled rye
½ lb. raisins
½ lb. (or more) raw wheat germ
Nuts, if desired
Millet can also be added or any other grain that appeals to you

Mix the various ingedients together in a very large container that has a tightly fitting cover. Use as a breakfast cereal (about ¾ cup or more per person) with raw apple or other fruit, milk, non-instant powdered milk, honey (if sweetening is absolutely necessary), and spoon plain or flavored yogurt on top.

ANTIPASTO SALAD
Yield: 12 servings

2½ c. chick-peas, cooked and drained
2 oz. anchovy fillets, drained
¼ lb. (or more) salami, cubed
6 oz. mozzarella cheese, cubed
12 stuffed olives
1 head lettuce, torn in bite-size pieces

4 stalks celery, chopped
1 onion, finely chopped
6 T. vegetable oil (or olive oil)
5 T. wine vinegar
1 t. salt
Freshly ground black pepper

In a large bowl, combine all ingredients except oil, vinegar, and seasonings. In a covered jar or blender, combine oil, vinegar, salt, and pepper to taste. Blend well and pour over chick-pea mixture. Toss carefully; correct seasonings. Garnish with parsley or chives, as desired.

Note: You can make ahead if you keep lettuce out until the last moment; then add and toss lightly.

Salads

"ANYTHING GOES" NUTRITIONAL TOSSED SALAD
(Yield: 8 servings)

6 c. greens (watercress, chicory, curly endive, Boston lettuce, collards, Chinese cabbage, escarole, romaine, spinach, Belgian endive, chard, turnip, mustard, cabbage, etc.)

2 c. vegetables (cauliflowerets, green and red pepper strips, bean sprouts, alfalfa sprouts, celery and carrot strips, radishes, chopped raw turnips or beets, broccoli buds, raw zucchini or summer squash, edible pod peas, chopped raw Jerusalem artichokes, kohlrabi matchsticks, sliced water chestnuts, mushrooms, steamed artichoke hearts, etc.)

½ c. or more of cooked, dry beans, soy bits, anchovies, sardines, leftover cooked vegetables or meat or poultry

½ c. or more garnishes (parsley, chives, thyme, wheat germ, horseradish, hard-boiled eggs, tarragon, basil, etc. Tomatoes, quartered, and other juicy foods should be added last).

1 large clove garlic

4 T. olive or vegetable oil

2 T. wine or cider vinegar or lemon juice

¾ t. salt
  Freshly ground black pepper

¼ t. dry mustard

Thoroughly wash greens in cold, running water. Dry completely in a salad basket (by spinning) or with Turkish towel or paper towels. Store immediately in salad storage container or plastic bag and chill until ready to use. Select and prepare other ingredients of your choice. Chill. When ready to serve, thoroughly rub large salad bowl with garlic. Tear greens into bite-size pieces, and place into bowl. Pour oil over and toss with large serving fork and spoon until each leaf is lightly coated with oil. Pour on vinegar, sprinkle on salt, pepper, and mustard. Add other vegetables, fish, meat, poultry, and whatever you have. Toss gently so everything has dressing on it. Taste and correct seasonings. Garnish as desired and serve immediately.

MARINATED MUSHROOM OR ARTICHOKE HEART SALAD
Yield: 8 servings

1 pkg. frozen artichoke hearts or ½ lb. or more clean mushrooms
  Italian Marinade

7-8 c. salad greens

⅓ c. sliced radishes

1 medium red onion, thinly sliced
  Whole wheat croutons

If using artichoke hearts, cook according to package directions (until just tender), drain. Place chosen vegetable in a small bowl, pour marinade over, and refrigerate, covered. Let marinate several hours, tossing lightly from time to time. When ready to serve, place greens, radishes, and onion slices in a large salad bowl. Drain marinade from mushrooms or artichoke hearts. Pour the chosen vegetable on top of greens; toss lightly. Pour on drained marinade as desired until greens are perfectly coated. Serve immediately, garnished with croutons.

ITALIAN MARINADE
Yield: 1¼ cup

1 c. vegetable or olive oil (or a combination)

3 T. wine vinegar

1 T. freshly squeezed lemon juice

3 large cloves garlic, minced

¾ t. salt

½ t. white pepper

⅛ t. cayenne pepper

¼ t. dry mustard
  Dash bottled hot pepper sauce

Combine ingredients in a jar, tightly cover and shake thoroughly. Pour over mushrooms, artichoke hearts, steamed green beans, salad greens, or whatever, as a marinade or salad dressing. Chill before using as a salad dressing. Chill while marinating the vegetables.

WILTED LETTUCE OR SPINACH
Yield: 4 servings

8 c. spinach or lettuce leaves, torn into bite-size pieces
5 strips bacon
1 lemon *or* ¼ c. tarragon vinegar
½ c. chopped green onion
½ t. salt
Freshly ground black pepper

Place greens in a salad bowl. Fry bacon until brown; remove with slotted spoon and place on paper towel to drain. Crumble. Squeeze the lemon and pour desired amount of juice into bacon fat (over medium heat). Add onion and cook approximately 2 minutes. Pour dressing over greens, sprinkle with crumbled bacon, and toss lightly. Taste and salt and pepper. Toss lightly again and serve.

SALADE NICOISE
Yield: 8 servings

4 potatoes, cooked, peeled, and sliced
Mayonnaise
3-4 ripe tomatoes, quartered
3 c. lightly steamed green beans
1 7-oz. can white tuna, drained and flaked
½ c. olives
1 medium red onion, thinly sliced
1 green pepper, deseeded and sliced into rounds
3 stalks celery, sliced
3 hard-boiled eggs, quartered
1 head Boston lettuce leaves
Vinaigrette Dressing
½ c. minced parsley
1 T. fresh chopped basil
½ t. chopped chives
Anchovies

Mix enough mayonnaise with potatoes to coat thoroughly. Toss tomatoes lightly in a small amount of Vinaigrette Dressing. In a separate bowl, toss green beans in a small amount of Vinaigrette Dressing. Let marinate while preparing the rest of the salad; drain before adding to salad. When ready to serve, toss lettuce lightly in a small amount of Vinaigrette Dressing until leaves are barely coated. Place around the edge and bottom of the bowl, using all the leaves. Place tuna in the center of the bowl; arrange tomatoes, green beans, and potatoes around the outside in an interesting pattern. Decorate with olives, onion slices, green pepper rounds, celery, and eggs. Garnish with herbs and anchovies. Serve immediately with additional Vinaigrette Dressing.

VINAIGRETTE DRESSING
Yield: 1cup

¼ c. wine vinegar (or part lemon juice)
¾ c. olive or salad oil
¼ t. salt
½ t. dry mustard
Freshly ground black pepper
1 t. minced parsley
1 t. minced sweet basil
1 large clove garlic, minced (optional)

Place all ingredients in a jar; cover tightly and shake thoroughly. Shake again just before using.

MADRA'S EXOTIC CABBAGE SALAD
Yield: 6 servings

2 c. white cabbage, chopped
2 c. red cabbage, chopped
¼ c. lemon juice
¼ c. vegetable oil
½ t. salt
Freshly ground black pepper
½ c. mint leaves, chopped
Pomegranate seeds, as desired

Mix the cabbages together in a salad bowl. Combine lemon juice, oil, salt and pepper. Pour over the cabbage and toss lightly. Taste and correct seasonings. Garnish with mint leaves and pomegranate seeds. Chill before serving.

TABOULI
Yield: 10 to 12 servings

3 c. boiling water
1½ c. raw bulgur wheat (cracked wheat)
1⅔ c. fresh parsley, finely minced
¾ c. fresh mint, finely minced
¾ c. chopped green onion
¼ c. (or more) lemon juice
¼ c. vegetable oil
4 medium tomatoes, chopped
½ t. salt
Freshly ground black pepper

Pour boiling water over wheat and let stand about 30 minutes. Drain and squeeze dry. (Save liquid for soup or other purpose.) Transfer wheat to a large mixing bowl. Salt lightly to taste. Mix in parsley, mint, and onion, salting lightly to taste after each addition. Stir in lemon juice and oil. Lightly mix in the tomatoes, salting again to taste. Add pepper to taste. Serve in a large bowl, garnished with lettuce leaves. You could also garnish with chopped cucumber and black olives.

CLASSIC SALAD
Yield: 6 to 8 servings

⅓ large head romaine, torn into small pieces
⅓ large head iceberg lettuce, torn into small pieces
3 c. other greens: spinach, chard, mustard, turnip, etc., torn into small pieces
1¾ c. thinly sliced, raw zucchini
½ c. sliced radishes
½ c. sliced, fresh mushrooms
3 green onions, sliced, tops and all
½ green pepper, deseeded and cut into strips
Wine-Vinegar Salad Dressing
½ c. crumbled blue cheese (optional)

Combine greens, zucchini, radishes, mushrooms, onions, and green pepper in a large salad bowl. Pour on dressing as desired, toss lightly, sprinkle blue cheese over top. Serve immediately.

WINE-VINEGAR SALAD DRESSING
Yield: 1 cup

⅓ c. wine vinegar
⅔ c. olive or vegetable oil
¼ t. salt
Freshly ground black pepper
1 large clove garlic, minced
1 T. minced parsley
1 T. minced chives
Any other fresh herbs desired, minced

Place all the above ingredients in a jar, tightly cover, and shake. Taste and correct seasonings. Chill until needed.

PEANUT COLESLAW
Yield: 6 to 8 servings

5-6 c. shredded cabbage (chilled)
2 c. chopped apple (chilled)
½ c. raisins
½ c. peanuts
Mayonnaise

In a salad bowl, combine cabbage, apples, raisins, and peanuts. Stir in enough mayonnaise to moisten the ingredients. Taste and add any seasoning desired. Serve immediately.

JIM AND JOHN'S PANZANELLA
Yield: 4 to 6 servings

Day old, good quality French bread, dried in oven and broken up
Olive oil (don't spare)
Wine vinegar
Italian parsley (or regular, if unavailable), chopped
4 large leaves basil, chopped
Salt
Freshly ground black pepper
1 tomato, chopped
2 stalks celery, chopped
1 medium sweet red onion, thinly sliced
Capers

Combine bread, olive oil, vinegar, parsley, basil, salt, and pepper in a salad bowl. Toss gently until ingredients are well flavored. Add tomato, celery, onion, and capers. Toss again lightly and serve immediately.

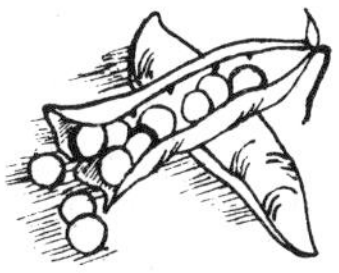

CURRIED VEGETABLE SALAD
Yield: 5 to 6 servings

1 c. broccoli buds, in bite-size pieces
1½ c. carrots, in bite-size pieces
1½ c. cauliflower florets
½ c. chopped green onion
Curry Marinade
Lettuce leaves (for garnish)

Steam vegetables, except green onions, lightly if they are not young and tender (or use blanched, frozen vegetables). Combine in a medium-size bowl; pour Marinade over. Cover and let marinate for about 12 hours, refrigerated. Toss lightly from time to time. When ready to serve, toss again and drain. Place in a salad bowl, garnished with lettuce or on individual serving plates.

CURRY MARINADE
Yield: ¾ cup

½ c. vegetable or olive oil
¼ c. cider vinegar
2 large cloves garlic, minced
½ t. salt
¼ t. cayenne pepper
1 T. curry powder

Combine ingredients and mix thoroughly. Pour over vegetables.

Note: This dish can also be used as an appetizer.

EMMA ROGERS' CHICKEN 'N' ORANGE SALAD
Yield: 6 to 8 servings

 3 c. chicken, cooked and diced
 1 c. diced celery
 1 c. diced pineapple
 1 c. orange sections, halved
 ⅛ t. salt
 2 T. vegetable oil
 2 T. orange juice
 2 T. white vinegar
 ⅛ t. rosemary
 ⅛ t. marjoram
 ⅛ t. thyme
 ½ c. mayonnaise
 ½ c. walnuts, chopped
 1 c. green grapes
   Lettuce

In a large bowl, combine all ingredients but mayonnaise, walnuts, and green grapes. Let marinate for one hour; drain and stir in mayonnaise. Taste and correct seasonings. Finally stir in nuts and grapes. Serve, accompanied by lettuce leaves.

TOMATO AND SHRIMP SALAD
Yield: 4 servings

 4 tomatoes, cut in eighths
2½ T. olive oil
 1 T. lemon juice
 1 T. minced fresh herbs (parsley, tarragon, chives)
 1 T. minced green onion
 8 oz. small, cooked shrimp (peeled and deveined)
   Salt
   Freshly ground black pepper
   Lettuce
 ⅓ c. (or more) toasted wheat germ

Put tomatoes into a bowl. Mix olive oil and lemon juice together; stir in herbs and onions. Pour over tomatoes. Add shrimp, combining gently. Check for seasonings and add salt and pepper as desired. Let salad marinate at room temperature for 30 minutes; then chill. When ready to serve, place lettuce leaves attractively on 4 plates. Saving a few shrimp for garnishing, divide the rest of the mixture among the four plates. Sprinkle wheat germ on each salad. Garnish with reserved shrimp and parsley.

FOUR BEAN SALAD
Yield: 12 servings

 2 c. cooked red kidney beans, drained
 2 c. cooked green beans, drained
 2 c. cooked chick-peas, drained
 2 c. cooked wax beans, drained
 1 large onion, thinly sliced
 1 large green pepper, thinly sliced
 2 T. honey
 2 t. salt
   Freshly ground black pepper
 ½ c. vegetable or olive oil
 ½ c. cider vinegar
   Lettuce

Reserve cooking liquids from beans for soup or other purpose. Slice green and wax beans if they are not already sliced. In a large bowl, combine all beans and vegetables, except lettuce. In a covered jar or blender, combine honey, salt, pepper, oil, and vinegar. Blend well and pour over bean mixture. Toss carefully; correct seasonings. Chill overnight or until flavors are well blended. Serve garnished with lettuce, parsley, and chives, if desired.

Note: This is an excellent dish in which to use up your canned green and yellow beans.

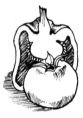

GRANDMA EARLE'S HOT GERMAN POTATO SALAD
Yield: 6 servings

 6 strips bacon
1½ c. chopped onion
 4 c. cooked potato, peeled and sliced
 2 T. cider vinegar
   Salt
   Freshly ground black pepper
   Parsley, minced
   Tomatoes, quartered (optional)

Fry bacon until crisp; remove with a slotted spoon and let drain on paper towel. Pour off excess bacon fat, if necessary, reserving about ¼ cup in frying pan. Add onion and cook until just transparent. Add potatoes and toss lightly. When potatoes are heated through, add vinegar to taste. Add salt and pepper as desired. Serve hot, garnished with fresh parsley and tomatoes, if desired.

YOGURT
Yield: 4 cups

Unbelievable as it may sound, once you know your milk (it should come from cows which have not been given antibiotics), have a thermometer which will register from 115° to 190° F., and have an ideal incubator (commercial "yogurt makers" have come down in price and are excellent, but they are not necessary), yogurt making itself is extraordinarily easy. You don't necessarily need an expensive yogurt culture for a starter, either. Good quality, commercial plain yogurt will do, if fresh.

½ c. non-instant powdered milk
1 qt. milk
3 T. plain yogurt from a high quality commercial yogurt

Heat the milks in a heavy-bottomed pan to near boiling (190°), then cool to 115°. Stir the yogurt in thoroughly; pour mixture into sterile, pre-warmed jars with tight-fitting lids. (Large baby food jars, pint jars, etc. do well.) Put jars on a rack in an electric pan. Fill with 115° water to just below the jar brims. (Or see below for other incubating methods.) Keep water temperature at an even 115°. If it goes above 120° the culture could be killed. As soon as the yogurt reaches the consistency of pudding, refrigerate immediately, or you, like Little Miss Muffet, will have to eat curds and whey.

Note: You can use your own yogurt as the starter until you notice that results aren't as good as you would wish. Then start again with commercial plain yogurt.

Other incubators: If your oven will maintain an even 115°, place the jars in pan filled to the jar brims with 115° water and place the whole business in the oven. A deep-fat fryer, electric frying pan, or the pilot light on the stove all could work for you. Also self-incubation: pour the yogurt mixture into a sterile quart jar, tightly wrap in many towels and put somewhere warm for 6 to 8 hours (where it won't be disturbed or jostled).

CUCUMBERS IN YOGURT WITH MINT
Yield: 6 servings

1 large cucumber, chopped (peeled, if necessary, and deseeded)
2 c. plain yogurt, whipped
⅛ t. chili powder
⅛ t. dry mustard
¾ t. salt
   Freshly ground black pepper
½ c. chopped mint leaves

Let cucumber drain for about ½ hour in colander. Reserve juices for soup or other purpose. Place yogurt and seasonings in a medium-size bowl. Mix lightly and stir in cucumber. Correct seasonings. Chill until served. Garnish with mint.

Note: Especially good with curries.

EASY FRUIT AND YOGURT
Yield: About 4 servings

1 orange, peeled, sectioned, and halved
1 large apple, cored and sliced
1 banana, sliced
1 c. seedless grapes
   Strawberry, raspberry, cherry flavored yogurt (or your choice)
   Add any other fruit you desire or substitute for the above.

Mix fruits together and gently fold in yogurt until fruits are covered. Add raisins, nuts, or seeds, wheat germ, etc. and garnish with lettuce, if desired. (Can also be used as a dessert.)

CREAM AND LEMON SALAD DRESSING
Yield: About ¾ cup

   Juice of ½ lemon
2½ T. olive or vegetable oil
   5 T. cream (more, if you wish)
   1 t. catsup
   1 t. prepared mustard
¼ c. minced onion
   2 T. chopped parsley
   1 sprig tarragon, chopped
   Salt
   Freshly ground black pepper

Mix ingredients in a jar; tightly cover and shake well. Serve over washed, dried, chilled salad greens which have been torn into serving pieces. Toss well and add quartered tomatoes.

Sauces and Condiments

FRESH TOMATO SAUCE
Yield: 2½ cups

- 3-4 garlic cloves, minced
- ½ c. onion
- 3 T. butter
- 8-10 very ripe tomatoes, unpeeled and chopped
- 3 fresh basil leaves chopped (or 1 t. dried)
- Salt
- Freshly ground black pepper

In a large frying pan over medium heat, sauté garlic and onion in butter for about 1 minute. Add tomatoes and cook briskly about 5 minutes. Lower heat, add basil, and continue to simmer until sauce is of desired consistency. Add salt and pepper to taste. Serve sauce over ¾ pound, cooked, whole wheat noodles, and pass Parmesan cheese. Or use in any dish calling for tomato sauce or freeze for later use.

FAVORITE TOMATO SAUCE WITH MEAT
Yield: 7 cups sauce

- 1 T. vegetable or olive oil
- 1 lb. ground beef
- ¾ c. chopped onion
- 3 cloves garlic, minced
- 4 c. canned tomatoes
- ¾ c. tomato paste
- 1 T. chopped parsley
- 1 t. salt
- Freshly ground black pepper
- ½ t. fennel or anise seed
- 1 t. sweet basil
- 1 t. oregano
- 2 T. freshly grated Parmesan cheese

In a large frying pan, cook the meat, onion, and garlic in the oil until beef is browned. Add the rest of the ingredients and simmer, uncovered, about 1 hour. Taste and correct seasonings. Use as a spaghetti sauce, in eggplant or veal Parmesan dishes, in lasagna, or in any other dish that calls for a similar sauce.

MOM'S QUICK "WHITE" SAUCE MIX
Yield: Mix for 6 cups sauce

- 1⅓ c. non-instant powdered milk
- ¾ c. whole wheat flour
- 1 t. salt
- ½ c. margarine
- Freshly ground black pepper

Mix together milk, flour, and salt. With a pastry blender, cut in margarine until mixture resembles fine crumbs. Refrigerate in tightly covered container. To make 1 cup sauce, pour one cup cold milk into a small, heavy bottomed pan. Thoroughly stir in ½ cup of the mix. Stir regularly over medium heat until mixture is thickened and bubbly. Grind black pepper in to taste.

HORSERADISH SAUCE
Yield: About 1 pint

- 1 lb. or more horseradish roots, thoroughly washed
- 1¾ c. vinegar
- 1 t. salt

Use a vegetable brush and hot water to clean the roots, if necessary. Scrape the skin off the roots and grate or put through a heavy-duty meat grinder. Mix salt and vinegar; add grated horseradish and mix together thoroughly. Cover tightly and refrigerate until needed.

MINT SAUCE
Yield: About ¾ cup

- 3 T. water
- 2 t. honey
- ⅓ c. finely chopped mint leaves
- ¼ c. cider vinegar

In a heavy-bottomed, small pan, heat water and honey until thoroughly mixed. Cool and add the mint leaves and the vinegar. Taste and adjust seasonings as you wish. Chill. Serve with lamb.

COTTAGE CHEESE
Yield: About 1 cup

1 qt. skimmed milk
1 rennet tablet
1 T. cold water
½ c. yogurt
½ t. salt

Pour milk into a heavy pan and heat over medium heat until lukewarm (110°). Meanwhile, crush rennet tablet into water. When milk reaches 110°, turn off heat, stir in rennet mixture, and let stand for 10 minutes or until mixture is set. Cover and cook over very low heat (maintain the mixture at 110°) stirring gently every five minutes or so. When curd becomes firm and has separated itself from the whey (20 to 30 minutes), pour into a colander lined with a fine, clean cloth (a piece of sheet works well, as does fine cheesecloth). Pick up corners of cloth occasionally, so all the whey has a chance to drain off. When curd is well drained, pour into a small, covered refrigerator dish; stir in yogurt and salt. Let stand at least ½ hour before serving. Serve plain or with chives, pineapple, or other favorite addition. Use in dishes requiring cottage cheese, such as blintzes, Red 'n' White Casserole, etc.

MAYONNAISE
Yield: 1 cup

Have all ingredients at room temperature:

1 egg yolk
¾ t. salt
¼ t. ground white pepper (or black)
½ t. dry mustard
½ t. paprika
2 T. lemon juice or vinegar
1 c. vegetable oil

Put yolk and seasonings in blender. Cover and turn on low speed. Blend until yolk is thick and foamy. Blend in 1 tablespoon lemon juice. Very gradually, drop by drop, pour in half of the vegetable oil. As mayonnaise thickens, run at high speed. Occasionally, stop the blender and scrape sides. Add the rest of the lemon juice. Very gradually, while blender continues on high, pour in remaining vegetable oil. Pour into clean jar, cover tightly, and refrigerate.

TOMATO PASTE
(OR PURÉE)
Yield: About 2 pints

8 lbs. ripe Italian plum tomatoes, chopped
1 t. salt
1 stalk celery and leaves, chopped
½ c. chopped onion
1 T. chopped parsley
1 t. oregano
½ t. sweet basil
1 large clove garlic, minced
4 whole cloves
½ t. black peppercorns
½ t. cinnamon

In a large, heavy bottomed pan, simmer the above ingredients until tomatoes are tender, stirring frequently. Sieve the mixture and place pulp back in heavy bottomed pan (or in the top of a double boiler). Stir frequently to avoid scorching. Continue to simmer until mixture is of the desired consistency. Pack into hot, sterilized jars; seal at once.

TOMATO CATSUP
Yield: 4 to 5 pints

2 c. white vinegar
1 t. cinnamon
1 T. whole cloves
2 t. celery seed
½ t. cayenne pepper
15-16 lbs. ripe tomatoes, washed and quartered
1 c. chopped onion
3 large cloves garlic, minced
1½ c. brown sugar
2 T. salt

Place vinegar and spices into a medium-sized pan; cover and bring to a boil. Remove from heat and let cool. Place tomatoes in a large, heavy-bottomed pan; add onion and garlic and bring to the boil. Cook about 15 minutes, stirring occasionally, or until tomatoes are soft. Strain tomatoes and put pulp back into the heavy-bottomed pan. Add sugar, bring to a boil and simmer until reduced by about half. Strain the vinegar mixture into the tomato pulp, discarding spices. Add salt and simmer, stirring regularly, until of desired consistency. Taste and correct seasonings. Pour into hot, sterilized jars and seal at once.

MRS. ROGERS'
RIPE TOMATO RELISH
Yield: About 8 pints

- 10 lbs. ripe tomatoes, blanched, peeled, and chopped
- 3 c. diced celery
- ¾ c. diced green pepper
- ¾ c. chopped onion
- ½ c. finely grated horseradish
- ⅔ c. salt
- 4-7 c. sugar
- 3 T. mustard seed
- 1½ c. cider vinegar
- 2 t. cinnamon

Combine vegetables and salt in a large bowl; let stand overnight in refrigerator. Drain, reserve salty liquid for another purpose. Mix vegetables with rest of the ingredients, adding sugar to taste. Keeps 6 months or longer in covered jars in refrigerator. Excellent with beef fondue, on top of hamburgers, or as a side dish.

GREEN TOMATO CHUTNEY
Yield: About 3 pints

- 1½ c. brown sugar, firmly packed
- 2 c. cider vinegar
- 2 lbs. chopped green tomatoes
- 2 c. chopped onion
- 2 tart apples, chopped
- ¼ c. chopped green chilies
- 1 c. seedless raisins
- ½ t. salt

In a heavy saucepan over medium hot heat, bring sugar and vinegar to a boil. Lower heat and simmer 5 minutes or more. Meanwhile, prepare fruits and vegetables. Add slowly, in order. Simmer until everything is tender and chutney is of the desired consistency. (This can take several hours.) Stir regularly during the cooking. Taste and correct seasonings. This mixture will last a long time refrigerated, or you could can it in pint jars using the hot water bath method.

Desserts

SOURDOUGH CHOCOLATE CAKE
Yield: 16 servings

½ c. sourdough starter (see index)
1 c. lukewarm water
1½ c. whole wheat flour
¼ c. non-instant powdered milk
1 c. brown sugar
½ c. margarine
1 T. nutritional yeast
1 T. soy flour
½ t. salt
1 t. cinnamon
1½ t. baking soda
⅓ c. cocoa
2 T. vegetable oil
1 t. vanilla
2 eggs

Mix starter, water, flour and powdered milk together in a warmed mixing bowl. Let ferment 2 to 3 hours in a warm place until mixture is bubbly. Preheat oven to 350°. Cream together sugar and margarine until light and fluffy. Add yeast, soy flour, salt, cinnamon, soda, cocoa, oil, and vanilla. Stir until well blended. Beat in eggs one at a time. When thoroughly mixed, combine chocolate mixture with sour dough mixture. Stir until thoroughly blended. Pour into two well-greased layer cake pans or an 11¼ x 7½ x 1½-inch cake pan. Bake for 25 to 30 minutes or until center springs back when pressed lightly. Cool thoroughly before removing from pan.

YOGURT-CRUMB CAKE
Yield: 16-20 pieces of cake

½ c. margarine
1½ c. brown sugar
2 c. whole wheat flour, sifted
¼ c. soy flour
1 egg
1 c. sour milk or yogurt
1 baking soda
¼ t. cloves
¼ t. cinnamon
½ t. salt

Preheat oven to 350°. With a pastry blender cut brown sugar and flours into shortening until mixture resembles crumbs. Set aside one cup of mixture. To remainder of crumb mixture, add remaining ingredients and beat thoroughly. Spoon into a greased 9 x 15-inch pan. Sprinkle reserved crumb mixture on top. Bake for about 30 minutes or until cake springs back when touched lightly.

Note: You can also bake this cake in a 9 x 9-inch pan. Increase the baking time.

PUMPKIN CAKE
Yield: 16-24 slices

1 c. unbleached white flour
2 c. whole wheat flour
¼ c. wheat germ
2 t. baking powder
2 t. baking soda
2 t. cinnamon
1 t. freshly ground nutmeg
1 t. salt
2 c. brown sugar, firmly packed
1¼ c. vegetable oil
1⅓ c. pumpkin purée, fresh or canned
4 eggs
¾ c. seedless raisins
¾ c. golden raisins
1½ c. chopped walnuts, pecans, or
      other nuts

Preheat oven to 350°. Mix together the first 8 dry ingredients. Set aside. Place the sugar, oil, and pumpkin purée in a large mixing bowl and beat well at medium speed. Add the eggs, one at a time, beating well after each addition. Fold dry ingredients into the wet ingredients. Finally, stir in raisins and nuts.

Pour into a well-greased 10-inch bundt or tube pan. Bake 1¼ hours or until done. Cake will be brown in color. Let cool 10 minutes in pan before turning out onto a rack. Can be frozen very successfully at this point. When serving, sprinkle with confectioners' sugar and, if desired, ground nuts.

CARROT CUSTARD
Yield: 6 servings

1 lb. carrots, pared and cut into 1-inch pieces (or 1 lb. cooked yellow summer or winter squash or pumpkin)
1 c. milk
½ c. non-instant powdered milk
3 eggs, beaten
½ c. light brown sugar
1 t. lemon rind
½ t. cloves (or allspice)
1 t. cinnamon
1 t. nutmeg
⅛ t. salt

Preheat oven to 350°. Place carrots in 1 cup boiling water; cover tightly and cook until tender. Drain. Purée carrots in blender with milk and milk powder. Pour into a medium-sized bowl. Add remaining ingredients and beat until blended. Pour into six ⅔-cup buttered custard or tea cups. Place in a shallow baking dish. Pour boiling water into dish to a depth of one inch. Bake 35 to 40 minutes or until knife inserted in center comes out clean. Serve warm or chilled. Garnish with wheat germ if desired.

APRICOT NUT BARS
Yield: 12-16 bars

¾ c. dried apricots (or other dried fruit: raisins, prunes, dates, peaches)

SHORTBREAD

1 c. whole wheat pastry flour
¼ c. brown sugar, firmly packed
¼ c. wheat germ
½ c. butter or margarine

Put apricots in a small pan and cover with water. Over medium heat, cook until tender (tightly covered). Drain (keep juice for other purpose), cool, and chop into small pieces. Preheat oven to 325°

In small bowl, mix together flour, brown sugar, and wheat germ. Cut in butter with a pastry blender until mixture resembles crumbs. Pat into a square 9 x 9-inch baking pan and bake 25 minutes or until lightly browned.

Spread Topping over hot, baked layer and put in oven again for about 35 minutes or until toothpick inserted in center comes out clean. Cool in pan before slicing into bars.

TOPPING

2 eggs, well beaten
1 c. firmly packed brown sugar
½ t. baking powder
⅓ c. whole wheat flour
½ t. salt
½ t. vanilla
½ c. chopped walnuts

Combine eggs and 1 cup brown sugar. Stir in apricots and remaining ingredients.

BREAD PUDDING WITH EGG SAUCE
Yield: 6-8 servings

3-4 c. stale whole wheat bread cubes
3 eggs
1 qt. milk
⅓ c. honey
⅓ c. raw wheat germ
⅓ c. non-instant powdered milk
1 t. vanilla
¼ t. salt
¾ c. raisins
1 c. chopped nuts (optional)

Butter a 1½-2 quart baking dish and place bread cubes on the bottom. Preheat oven to 350°. In a large bowl, beat eggs until light and foamy; add milk, honey, wheat germ, powdered milk, vanilla and salt. Blend well and pour over bread cubes, allowing bread to soak thoroughly. Sprinkle raisins and nuts over the top of the pudding. Place dish in a flat pan, half filled with hot water and bake for about one hour or until knife inserted in center comes out almost clean. Serve hot with Egg Sauce.

EGG SAUCE

3 egg yolks
½ c. honey
½ t. vanilla
⅛ t. salt
½ t. nutmeg

Beat yolks until light and foamy; add remaining ingredients. Beat well until thoroughly blended. Serve cold over warm pudding.

57

WORDSWORTH GINGERBREAD
Yield: 12 slices

1¾ c. whole wheat pastry flour
¼ c. raw wheat germ
1 T. nutritional yeast
1 T. soy flour
2 t. ginger
¾ c. butter or softened margarine
¾ c. brown sugar
2 T. honey

Preheat oven to 325°. Mix together the dry ingredients, except brown sugar. Cut in butter with a pastry blender or with your fingertips until mixture resembles fine crumbs. Mix in brown sugar. Stir in honey. Press mixture into greased 8½-inch round cake pan and bake 45 to 50 minutes, until golden. Don't overbake. Let cool for about 15 minutes; then cut into 12 pieces and remove to a wire rack to finish cooling.

Note: This gingerbread is crisp and more like shortbread than cake.

HONEY-NUT BALLS
Yield: About 1½ dozen

½ c. sesame or non-hydrogenated peanut butter
¼ c. honey
½ c. or more non-instant powdered milk or soy milk powder
1 T. sunflower seeds
1 T. chopped walnuts
1 T. raisins or currants
3 T. sesame seeds

Mix peanut butter and honey until well blended. Gradually add powdered milk until mixture resembles bread dough. Stir in the rest of the ingredients, except sesame seeds. If more fruit or nuts are desired, add to taste. Roll mixture into small balls and roll in the sesame seeds. Refrigerate until needed.

SALTED PEANUT COOKIES
Yield: 3 dozen cookies

1 c. brown sugar
¾ c. softened margarine or butter
1 large egg
1 c. whole wheat flour
2 t. baking powder
¼ c. non-instant powdered milk
¼ c. raw wheat germ
1¾ c. rolled oats
1 c. salted peanuts

Preheat oven to 350°. Cream together margarine and sugar, beat in egg until fluffy. Mix dry ingredients together (except peanuts) and stir into egg mixture until thoroughly blended. Stir in peanuts. Drop by teaspoonfuls onto lightly greased cookie sheets and bake for 12 to 15 minutes or until top springs back when touched lightly. Do not burn!

MIXED-GRAIN COOKIES
Yield: 3 dozen cookies

½ c. brown sugar, firmly packed
½ c. margarine
1 egg
1 t. vanilla
4 t. milk
1¼ c. whole wheat flour
¼ c. soy flour
¼ c. raw wheat germ
½ t. baking soda
½ t. baking powder
½ t. salt
¾ c. uncooked mixed grains or muesli or oatmeal
½ c. raisins

Preheat oven to 350°. Cream margarine and sugar, beat in egg. Add vanilla and milk. Mix dry ingredients together thoroughly. Add all at once to egg mixture and mix well. Add raisins. Drop dough from teaspoon onto greased cookie sheets. Bake approximately 10 minutes or until lightly browned.

CARROT COOKIES
Yield: 6 dozen cookies

2½ c. whole wheat flour
¼ c. raw wheat germ
1 T. soy flour
1 T. nutritional yeast
1 t. salt
1 t. allspice
1 c. softened margarine
¾ c. brown sugar
2 eggs
1 c. grated raw carrots
1 T. grated orange rind
¾ c. currants (or raisins)
Chopped nuts, optional

Preheat oven to 375°. Mix first six dry ingredients together. Set aside. Cream margarine and brown sugar until light and fluffy; beat in eggs. Gradually stir in flour mixture and remaining ingredients. Bake a "test" cookie; add more flour if necessary for cookie to retain shape. Drop by teaspoonfuls onto greased baking sheets. Bake 10 to 12 minutes or until done. Cool on wire racks.

HEALTHFUL COOKING AND BAKING HINTS AND SUGGESTIONS

If you are new to natural, organically grown foods, you should know that increasing numbers of people are growing them in their own naturally composted gardens and/or are demanding them in specialty food stores. There has been a notable upsurge in the numbers of organic-food co-ops, health and whole food stores, macrobiotic, and vegetarian stores in the United States, not to mention special health-food sections in large supermarkets. The customer should be aware, however, that some of these stores are overcharging and sometimes misrepresenting their products; it is wise to get to know your supplier and his supplier as well, so you know you are getting what you are paying for.

It should also be pointed out that even though a person thinks he has done all the right things in growing or buying his own food, his cooking or handling methods could be killing natural nutrients. For example, nearly all vegetables should be cooked unpeeled, thinly sliced, and in the shortest time possible. They should be steamed or cooked with a tiny amount of boiling liquid such as the leftover vegetable water from another recent food preparation. Or they should be sautéed quickly as in Oriental cooking in a little vegetable oil. Salt, butter, or margarine should, generally speaking, not be added until just before serving. Most people know that fresh vegetables are more nutritious than those which have been stored, but many people do not know that vegetables should be kept refrigerated, unwashed, until immediately before they are to be used.

Here are some other things about natural foods you should know: Even if you're not worried about cholesterol, coconut and palm oil should be omitted from your diet. You should know that most imitation dairy products, most commercially baked goods, and most of the cake and other mixes on supermarket shelves are made with these oils which are high in saturated fats. If you want the best low cholesterol product, use safflower oil. Other nutritional oils are corn, cottonseed, peanut, and soybean oils and margarine which is called "liquid" on the label. Do not heat oils above 360° F.

When you purchase items such as margarine, peanut butter, or lard, do not buy those labeled hydrogenated. In the case of peanut butter, this will mean there will be natural separation of oil. If you stir the peanut butter well when you first open the jar and then put the jar immediately into the refrigerator, you won't be bothered by the oil separation.

Whole wheat flour should be bought and used as soon as possible after it has been stone ground. It, as well as wheat germ and other wheat products, unrefined vegetable oil, non-hydrogenated peanut butter, powdered milk, and a number of highly nutritious foods should be kept in a tightly covered container in the refrigerator to prevent loss of nutrients.

Such common foods as cheese, cottage cheese, milk, and eggs should be kept carefully covered at all times, including during cooking, to prevent nutritional loss.

So-called raw sugar has no more nutritional benefits than has refined white sugar. There is no use spending the extra money for the raw; do try to substitute molasses and honey for refined sugar whenever possible (see substitution chart). The recipes for desserts in this book include so many healthful ingredients that the use of some carefully chosen sweeteners seems somewhat justified.

You can get more calcium and protein into your food by adding non-instant powdered milk (which has twice the nutritional benefits of instant powdered milk). Non-instant milk blends quickly with other liquids when beaten with a mixer or put into a blender. Ways to add the benefits of powdered milk to your food:

    a. For each cup of milk in soups, sauces, and the like, add ¼ cup powder; for each cup of water or other liquid, add ½ cup powder.

    b. For each pound of ground meat in hamburgers, meat balls, etc., add up to ¾ cup powder.

    c. For each cup of milk in drinks made of milk, add up to ¼ cup powder.

    d. In many of your favorite recipes you can add ½ cup powdered milk with no difficulty; a little experimentation is fun and profitable for your health.

Another way to inexpensively get extra protein and vitamins is by adding raw wheat germ, nutritional yeast, or a small amount of soy flour or soy grits to food whenever possible.

Some of the places to go for unfamiliar ingredients in this book are health and whole food stores, oriental, middle Eastern, Italian, and Indian grocery stores, vegetarian shops, macrobiotic stores, or special health or ethnic food sections in supermarkets.

GLOSSARY OF TERMS USED IN THIS BOOK

Blanch - For tomatoes and such fruits and vegetables, this means pouring boiling water over them to make removal of the skins easier (should be done as seldom as possible). Otherwise, blanching generally means a method used before freezing vegetables: vegetables are dropped slowly in boiling water for a few minutes (different time for each vegetable) then immediately placed in ice water so cooking stops.

Bulgur or bulghur - Cracked wheat

Carob - A chocolate substitute made from the St. John's plant. The pod is crushed to a fine powder. It does not produce the allergic reactions that chocolate does.

Chick-peas - Another name for garbanzo beans

Chop - To cut into small pieces

Graham flour - Another name for whole grain or whole wheat flour. The best graham flour is stone ground because this process does not generate the heat that kills many of the nutrients.

Mince - To cut up into very fine, tiny pieces. In the case of garlic, a garlic press does the job very easily.

Nituke - Sautéed vegetables which are thinly sliced.

Non-hydrogenated - Preferable to hydrogenated foods like oils which are processed with hydrogen to produce a solid fat.

Non-instant - Non-instant powdered milk has more nutrients than instant; it is usually more satisfactory in baking than instant.

Nutritional yeast - Another name for brewer's yeast; will not help make food rise but has many nutrients and can be added to foods in small proportions to add protein and the vitamin B complex.

Old-fashioned molasses - Unsulphured, dark molasses.

Organically grown foods - Foods grown without chemical fertilizers or pesticides.

Purée - Mashed into a pulp after cooking — usually in a blender or in a sieve.

Raw wheat germ - Some of the nutrients in wheat germ are harmed by heat, so it is preferable to use raw wheat germ when possible. When you need toasted wheat germ, do it yourself in a 300° oven (mixed with a small amount of honey, if desired) for about 10 minutes.

Sauté - Quick cooking in a small amount of oil, turning frequently.

Sea salt - salt produced from seawater by evaporation.

Simmer - Cooking method whereby temperature is just at or below boiling point; bubbles rise gently to surface.

Steam - An excellent cooking method in which the food is never touched by water. Place a small amount of water in the bottom of a pan and place vegetables or what-have-you in a stainless steel steamer or on a rack. Cover the pan and the steam produced from the boiling water will do the cooking.

Tahini - Sesame butter, made from ground, hulled sesame seeds.

Tamari - A soy sauce concentrate available in natural food stores. Commercial soy sauce is not really a substitute.

Tempura - Deep-fried, battered foods.

Whole wheat flour - Flour ground from the whole grain, containing the endosperm, bran, and germ.

Whole wheat pastry flour - More finely ground than plain whole wheat flour.

Umeboshi plums - Not easy to find; they are Japanese in origin. They are plums preserved in salt for 3 years.

Unbleached flour - Creamy white flour which has not been bleached with chemicals.

SUBSTITUTIONS

If you wish to change some of your favorite recipes to make them more nutritious (or if you don't have an ingredient called for), check this substitution list. Don't be afraid to experiment:

1 cup buttermilk or sour cream = 1 cup yogurt

1 cup sour milk = 1 cup milk plus 1 T. vinegar or lemon juice (stir and let sit to "clabber") or use buttermilk

¼ cup cocoa = ¼ cup carob powder

1 cup granulated sugar (often too much sugar is called for in recipes — sometimes you can cut down greatly on sugar by adding pure vanilla extract) = 1 cup honey in yeast breads; ⅞ cup honey in cookies and cakes — reduce liquid in recipe by 3 T. or 1 cup firmly packed light brown sugar or 1 cup molasses or sorghum (does not work in every recipe) — reduce liquid in recipe by 3 T. or 1 cup maple syrup — reduce liquid in recipe by ¼ cup

1 cup all-purpose flour = 1¼ cups rye flour or ⅞ cup rice flour or ⅞ cup whole wheat flour or ⅞ cup cracked wheat or 1 cup unbleached flour or ⅔ cup whole wheat flour plus ⅓ cup wheat germ or ¾ cup whole wheat flour plus ¼ cup bran or ⅞ cup whole wheat flour plus 2 T. soy flour (reduce baking temperature about 25° when adding soy flour)

1 cup white, enriched, or converted rice = 1 cup brown rice

SX517 BOOK VIEWER STAND—This modern, see-through book stand, made of strong, durable Lucite, will protect books from smudges and dirt. Perfect for use in the kitchen, workshop, or study, the stand folds flat for easy and convenient storage or hanging. It's a great gift idea for only $4.00, plus $1.00 postage and handling. Order from Ideals Publishing Corporation, 11315 Watertown Plank Road, Milwaukee, WI 53226. Prices subject to change without notice.

IDEALS RECIPE CARD BOOKLETS—Each booklet contains thirty-two 3" x 5" recipe cards, perforated for easy removal. Booklets are available in two distinctive designs, each including a delicious recipe. Ideals Recipe Card Booklets may be purchased for $1.00 from your local bookstore.

Pictured opposite
Apricot Nut Bars, p. 57
Honey-Nut Balls, p. 59

Index